IN HONORE ET VIRTUTE.

Brownell

The

ANCESTORS

and

DESCENDANTS

of

Veranus Brownell

ITINERANT METHODIST PREACHER

೧೮೩೨೦೫

Lowell Lincoln Rogers

Heritage Books
2025

HERITAGE BOOKS

AN IMPRINT OF HERITAGE BOOKS, INC.

Books, CDs, and more—Worldwide

For our listing of thousands of titles see our website
at
www.HeritageBooks.com

A Facsimile Reprint
Published 2025 by
HERITAGE BOOKS, INC.
Publishing Division
5810 Ruatan Street
Berwyn Heights, MD 20740

International Standard Book Number
Paperbound: 978-0-7884-3055-8

DEDICATION

〔⊏═══════⊐〕

*This Book is Dedicated to the
Memory of*

VERANUS BROWNELL

And His Two Wives

MARGARET LEWIS JENKINS

AND

LOIS B. SHOWERS

Preface

The plan of this book is very simple. The charts show the ancestral lines of Veranus Brownell and Margaret Lewis Jenkins and Lois B. Showers. By following the numbers of the charts one may trace back the most of the lines of Veranus Brownell eight generations. The lines of Margaret Jenkins and Lois Showers are not traced so far.

At first the Brownell Line is given from Thomas Brownell the Immigrant down to Veranus Brownell. Short biographical sketches and the families of children in each generation follow.

Then we take up the Descendants of Veranus Brownell, and this is followed by the records of the Families who have married into the Brownell Family. These are arranged in alphabetical order.

VERANUS BROWNELL

See Chart No. 2	See Chart No. 3	See Chart No. 4	See Chart No. 5			See Chart No. 6	See Chart No. 7
1795 Portsmouth, R. I.	----	1781 Portsmouth, R. I.	1780	1759 Seige of Louisburg	----	--- in Ashford, Conn.	----
JOSEPH BROWNELL, SR. Lived in Pomfret, Vt. A Soldier in the Revolution.	REBECCA TRIPP Married Dec. 22, 1742	DAVID FISH Married Feb. 16, 1730	JEMIMA TALLMAN Portsmouth, R. I.	GEORGE CHEEDLE Lived in Lebanon, Conn.	MARTHA BURGE Married Aug. 6, 1721 in Lebanon, Conn.	DANIEL ALLEN	AZUBAH LADD Married Oct. 3, 1741
1720 Portsmouth, R. I.	1727 Portsmouth, R. I.	1710 Portsmouth, R. I.	1708	--- in England	--- in England	--- in Norwich, Conn.	1717

----		----		1805 in Pomfret, Vt.		1791 in Pomfret, Vt.	
NATHAN BROWNELL Soldier in the Revolution		ELIZABETH FISH Married Nov. 9, 1869		JOHN CHEEDLE A Soldier in the Revolution		RACHEL ALLEN Married 1869	
1747 in Portsmouth, R. I.		1747 in Portsmouth, R. I.		1732 in Lebanon, Conn.		1746 in Ashford, Conn.	

1770 in Portsmouth, R. I.	JOSEPH BROWNELL, JR.	---- in Pomfret, Vt. Married	1778 in Pomfret, Vt.	RACHEL CHEEDLE	1810 in Pomfret, Vt.
			June 11, 1809		

Born 1810 Pomfret, Vt.	VERANUS BROWNELL Married Nov. 19, 1833 (1st) Margaret Lewis Jenkins	Died 1874 Birdsall, N. Y.

CHART NO. 1

JOSEPH BROWNELL, SR.
Lived in Pomfret, Vt.
Married Rebecca Tripp

Born 1720 in Portsmouth, R. I.   Died 1795 in Portsmouth, R. I.

1690 — **JOSEPH BROWNELL** of Portsmouth, R. I. — ----

1697 — **RUTH CORNELL** of Portsmouth, R. I. — ----

Married Dec. 5, 1717

1646 — **GEORGE BROWNELL** of Portsmouth, R. I. Married Jan. 4, 1673 — 1738

1652 — **SUSANNA PIERCE** of Portsmouth, R. I. — 1744

1676 — **GEORGE CORNELL** of Portsmouth, R. I. — 1752

1679 — **PHILADELPHIA EASTIS** Married 1696 — 1752

1619 in England — **THOMAS BROWNELL** Portsmouth, R. I. — 1665

---- in England — **ANN ——** Married in England 1638 — 1665

1615 — **RICHARD PIERCE** Portsmouth, R. I. — 1678

1636 — **SUSANNA WRIGHT** — 1718

1653 — **THOMAS CORNELL** of Portsmouth, R. I. Married 1672 — 1714

1659 — **SUSANNA LAWTON** Portsmouth, R. I. — 1712

1645 — **MATTHEW EASTIS** Scituate, Mass. — 1721

1645 — **PHILADELPHIA JENCKS** Eliot, Maine — 1721

CHART NO. 2

JOHN TRIPP
Portsmouth, R. I.
1678 in Portsmouth, R. I.
1610 in England

MARY PAINE of Portsmouth, R. I.
1678

WILLIAM HALL of Dartmouth, Mass.
1675
1613 in England

MARY ———
1680

THOMAS WAIT of Portsmouth, R. I.
1677
1601

ELEANOR ———

JOHN LOUNDERS

JANE KIRBY

ABIAL TRIPP of Dartmouth, Mass. Married, 1679
1684
1653

DELIVERANCE HALL of Dartmouth, Mass.

REUBEN WAIT of Portsmouth, R. I. Married, 1681
1707

TABITHA LOUNDERS
1707

1684   **ABIAL TRIPP** of Portsmouth, R. I.   ----
Married

1688   **ELEANOR WAIT** of Portsmouth, R. I.   ----
1704

Born 1727
Portsmouth
R. I.

REBECCA TRIPP
Married Dec. 22, 1742
Joseph Brownell, Sr.

Died ----

CHART NO. 3

ROBERT FISH 1593 in England 16.9

ALICE FISH 1597 in England

WILLIAM HALL Dartmouth, Mass. 1613 1675

MARY —— 1680

JOHN TRIPP Portsmouth, R. I. 1610 1678

MARY PAINE Portsmouth, R. I. 1678

THOMAS FISH of Portsmouth, R. I. 1619 — 1699

MARY SHERMAN

ZURIAL HALL Portsmouth, R. I. — 1691

ELIZABETH TRIPP Portsmouth, R. I. 1648 — 1701

| ---- | ROBERT FISH of Portsmouth, R. I. | 1730 | ---- | MARY HALL of Portsmouth, R. I. | ---- |
| | | Married | 1686 | | |

| Born 1710 Portsmouth. R. I. | DAVID FISH Married Jemima Tallman | Died 1781 Portsmouth, R. I. |

CHART NO. 4

SAMUEL BRIGGS — 1685 .... ----

RICHARD SWAIN
Nantucket, R. I. — 1717 — Rowley, Mass. / 1601

ELIZABETH ———

NATHANIEL WYER
Nantucket, R. I. — 1717 — 1681 / ----

SARAH ———

PETER TALLMAN — 1708 .... ---

JOAN BRIGGS — 1685 .... ---

Married 1665

JOHN SWAIN
of
Nantucket, R. I. — 1717 .... ---

MARY WYER
of
Nantucket, R. I. — 1717 1633

| ---- | JAMES TALLMAN | 1724 | ---- | HANNAH SWAIN of Nantucket, R. I. | 1765 Sept. |

Married   Oct. 14, 1701

| 1708 Sept. | JEMIMA TALLMAN | 1780 |

Married, 1730

David Fish

CHART NO. 5

1632	1700

SAMUEL ALLEN
Bridgewater, Mass.

SARAH PARTRIDGE — 1634 / 1680

JOHN CARY
Bridgewater, Mass.
Married 1644 — 1622 / 1680

ELIZABETH GODFREY — --- / ---

RICHARD BUSHNELL
Married 1648 — --- / 1659

MARY MARVIN — 1629 / 1713

THOMAS LEFFINGWELL
Norwich, Conn. — --- / 1693

MARY BUSHNELL — --- / 1694

SAMUEL
ALLEN
Bridgewater, Mass.
Married 1685 — --- / ---

REBECCA
CARY
of
Bridgewater, Mass. — 1665 / 1697

JOSEPH
BUSHNELL
of
Norwich, Conn.
Married 1673 — 1651 / 1746

MARY
LEFFINGWELL
of
Norwich, Conn. — 1654 / 1745

| 1691 in Bridgewater, Mass. | TIMOTHY ALLEN | ---- Norwich, Conn. Married | 1699 | RACHEL BUSHNELL of Norwich, Conn. | ---- |
| | | 1714 | | | |

Born 1717	DANIEL ALLEN	----
Norwich,	Married, 1741	Ashford,
Conn.	Azubah Ladd	Conn.

CHART NO. 6

DANIEL LADD
of
Haverhill, Mass.   1693   ---

ANN ——   ---   ---

GEORGE CORLISS
Haverhill, N. H.
Married 1645   1686   1617 in England

JOANNA DAVIS   ---   ---

EDWARD HAZEN
Rowley, Mass.
Married 1650   1683   ---

HANNA GRANT   1715   ---

THOMAS HOWLETT
Ipswich, Mass.   ---   ---

SAMUEL LADD
Haverhill, N. H.
Married 1694   1698   1649

MARTHA CORLISS   ---   ---

THOMAS HAZEN
Rowley, Mass.
Married 1683   1735   1658

MARY HOWLET
of
Ipswich, Mass.   ---   ---

1698   DAVID LADD
of
Haverhill, N. H.   ----   ----   HEPZIBAH HAZEN
of
Rowley, Mass.   1728

Married   Oct. 1, 1716

1717   AZUBAH LADD
Haverhill, N. H.
Married, 1741, Daniel Allen   ----

CHART NO. 7

1791	RICHARD	1853	1799	ANN	----
in	LEWIS	Place		MARIA	
Yorks-	JENKINS	Un-		LEAKE	in
shire,		known			Burr Oak,
England					Mich.
		Married	Nov. 30, 1810		

1814	MARGARET LEWIS JENKINS	1853
in	Married, Nov. 19, 1833	in
Waterloo, N. Y.	Veranus Brownell	Birdsall, N. Y.

CHART NO. 8

----	WILLIAM	----	----	CATHERINE	----
	SHOWERS			MILLS	

1828	LOIS SHOWERS	1906
	of Urbana, N. Y.	
	She married Aug. 11, 1853,	
	Veranus Brownell	

CHART NO. 9

BROWNELL

0========0

I. THOMAS BROWNELL was born in Derbyshire, England, in 1619. His wife's name was ANN ————. There seems to be no record of her last name. They were married in 1638 and came to this country the following year. Austin in his Genealogical (?) Dictionary of Rhode Island states that he was the son of Sir Edmund Brownell of Derbyshire. The Brownells of Rhode Island possessed plate upon which was engraved the Coat of Arms, as presented upon the preceeding page, which was the Coat of Arms of the Brownell Family of Derbyshire. That he came to this country soon after their marriage is evidenced by the fact that they are found in Aquidneck in 1647, a small settlement at the North-end of Rhode Island now known as Portsmouth. This settlement had been formed nine years before this date by a little group of men and women who had been driven out of Boston because "Mr. and Mrs. Hutchinson had seduced them into dangerous errors." Here in Aquidneck had been signed that famous compact, as important as that other compact signed on tthe Mayflower. It was as follows:

> "The seventh of the first month in the year 1638, We, whose names are underwritten, do hereby solemnly, in the presence of Jehovah, incorporate ourselves into a bodie politick, and as He shall help us, will submit ourselves, our lives, and our estates, unto our Lord of Lords, and to all those perfect and most absolute Laws of His, given us in His Holy Word of Truth, to be guided and judged thereby. Ex. XXIV 2 & 3 and II Chron. II 3, and II Kings II 17."

This compact was signed by fourteen members of the Boston Church, twelve of whom had been required to give up their arms, in the previous year on account of their adherence to the doctrines of Mrs. Ann Hutchinson. It was among these people, who had been driven from Massachusetts on account of their religious opinions, that Thomas Brownell cast his lot.   We may judge somewhat of his character by his choice of the people among whom he decided to make his home.   His father, SIR EDMUND BROWNELL, was at one time Mayor of Coventry and held other most important positions.   The crest above the Coat of Arms bears emblems which indicate royal connections, or ancestors who were Noblemen.   The earliest record of his name in Portsmouth is under date ·of March 10, 1647, when he witnessed the will of John Walker, his neighbor on the South.   Thomas and Ann had four children born in England and four born in this country as follows:

1. MARY BROWNELL, born 1639, died 1739.   Married ROBERT HAZARD. Issue: Five children.
2. SARAH BROWNELL, born 1641, died 1676.   Married 1658 GIDEON FREE-BORN.   Issue: Seven children.
3. MARTHA BROWNELL, born 1643, died 1744. Married (1) JEREMIAH WAIT, (2) CHARLES DYER.
4. GEORGE BROWNELL, born 1646, died 1718.   Married SUSANNA PIERCE. For record see below.
5. WILLIAM BROWNELL, born 1648, died 1715.   Married SARAH SMITON. Issue: Elevent children.
6. THOMAS BROWNELL, born 1650, died 1732.   Married 1678 MARY PIERCE.   Issue: Six children.
7. ROBERT BROWNELL, born 1652, died 1728.   Married MARY ————. Issue: Six children.
8. ANN BROWNELL, born 1654, died 1747.   Married JOSEPH WILBUR. Issue: Nine children.

A remarkable family, eight children all of whom lived to be married and have children, large families, too.   It is also to be noted that two of them, viz Nos. 1 and 3, were 100 and 101 years old, respectively.   They all lived in Portsmouth, R. I., and the vital records of that place contain all the above data. Five years after landing in this country Thomas Brownell was made a freeman, i.e. he was given the rights of franchise.   He also held many important political offices and always acquitted himself with honor and merit.   It is a matter of just pride on the part of his descendants to know that the first one by the name of "Brownell" to live in this land was a man of religious character, and one to be honored by his compeers with many offices of trust.   He died in the year 1665 at the age of 46.   His wife, Ann, also passed away the same year. One might be led to wonder why they should have died so young. But in all probability the mystery would be solved if we could know the hardships and trials, sufferings and sacrifices incident to migration to a new land, to pioneer life, and the struggle to raise a large family of children. Savage says that Thomas Brownell was the Progenitor of all the Brownells in this country, except those who may have come over recently.

II. GEORGE BROWNELL, No. 4 above. Born 1646; died 1718. Married SUSANNA PIERCE. (See Pierce Family.) She was born 1652 and died 1743. Their children were:

1. SUSANNA BROWNELL, born 1675, died ————.
2. SARAH BROWNELL, born 1681.
3. MARY BROWNELL, born 1683.
4. MARTHA BROWNELL, born 1685.
5. THOMAS BROWNELL, born 1688.
6. JOSEPH BROWNELL, born 1690. Married 1717 RUTH CORNELL.
7. WAITE BROWNELL, born 1693.
8. STEPHEN BROWNELL, born 1695.

III. JOSEPH BROWNELL, No. 6 above. Lived in Portsmouth, R. I. He married, January 5, 1717, RUTH CORNELL, daughter of GEORGE CORNELL and PHILADELPHIA EASTIS, of Portsmouth, R. I. Their children were:

1. GEORGE BROWNELL, born 1718, died 1730.
2. JOSEPH BROWNELL, born 1720, died 1795. Married 1742 REBECCA TRIPP.
3. THOMAS BROWNELL, born 1722, died 1806.
4. WAITE BROWNELL, born 1724.
5. PHILADELPHIA BROWNELL, born 1726.
6. MARTHA BROWNELL, born 1728.
7. GEORGE BROWNELL, born 1736.

IV. JOSEPH BROWNELL, No. 2 above. Lived in Portsmouth, R. I. He married, December 22, 1742, REBECCA TRIPP, daughter of ABIAL TRIPP and ELEANOR WAITE, of Portsmouth, R. I. They had ten children, as follows:

1. STEPHEN BROWNELL, born 1744, died 1815.
2. JONATHAN (Capt.) BROWNELL, born 1746.
3. NATHAN BROWNELL, born 1747. Married ELIZABETH FISH.

4. OLIVER BROWNELL, born 1749.
5. PHILADELPHIA BROWNELL, born 1752. Married RICHARD SISSON.
6. SUSANNA BROWNELL, born 1745. Married GILES SLOCUM.
7. MARY BROWNELL, born 1757.
8. AMY BROWNELL, born 1760. Married BENJAMIN WEAVER.
9. THOMAS BROWNELL, born 1762. Married MERCY SHAW.
10. REBECCA BROWNELL, born 1765. Married JACOB MANN.

V. NATHAN BROWNELL, No. 3 above. Lived in Portsmouth, R. I. Married, November 9, 1769, ELIZABETH FISH, daughter of DAVID FISH and JEMIMA TALLMAN, of Portsmouth, R. I. Nathan and his father, Joseph, were both soldiers in the Revolutionary War. Their children were:

1. JOSEPH BROWNELL, born 1770. Married 1809 RACHEL CHEEDLE.
2. MARTHA BROWNELL, born 1773.
3. PATIENCE BROWNELL, born 1775.
4. CHARITY BROWNELL, born 1776.
5. ELIZABETH BROWNELL, born 1778.
.6 SUSANNA BROWNELL, born 1780.

VI. JOSEPH BROWNELL, No. 1 above. Was born in Portsmouth, R. I. Sometime, I have not found out when, he removed to Pomfret, Vt. Whether he came directly, or stopped somewhere else before coming to Vermont, I do not know. Owing to the fact that the home lot (now abandoned entirely) was about the most undesirable, looks as though he was a late arrival there and had to take what was left. He married in Pomfret, Vt., RACHEL CHEEDLE, June 11, 1809. She was the daughter of JOHN CHEEDLE and RACHEL ALLEN. The records of Pomfret show the presence of two Josephs, designated "Sr." and "Jr." The one called "Sr." must have been the Grandfather of the one called "Jr." The names, Philadelphia (a very unusual name, especially for girls) and Eleanor (both of which we find in the records of Pomfret and the latter one we find in Veranus' family of children) make me feel sure that this is the correct line. Joseph and Rachel had only one son:

1. VERANUS BROWNELL, born March 16, 1810, in Pomfret, Vt. RACHEL BROWNELL died March 26, 1810.

VII. VERANUS BROWNELL, No. 1 above. The only child of Joseph Brownell and Rachel Cheedle. Misfortune seems to

have been his birthright. Left motherless in infancy, it was
his hard lot, for the first eight years of his life to be cast among
people who had for him little sympathy and less care. He knew
not what it was to be loved. He was repeatedly and roughly
told "He was nothing but a worthless idiot, and would never
be anything but a fool." He suffered cruel violence at the
hands of the inhuman wretch who stood to him as "foster
father." At one time a rope was tied around his wrists and he
was drawn up until his toes barely touched the floor and then
was whipped until pools of blood had dripped from his lacer-
ated person. He was taken down in an insensible condition and
for many days it was not thought that he would recover. From
the effects of these brutalities he never fully escaped. Their
crushing influence hung like a hideous spell over all his earlier
years, and to the last it was manifested in an extremely modest
estimate of his own abilities and worth. This, together with
his generous and genuine application of the Apostolical precept,
"in honor preferring one another," may account for the humble
place he held in conference work. Some time after the death
of his mother, his father settled in Parishville, St. Lawrence
Co., N. Y., where he married again, Ruth ———. This
good, kind step-mother, learning of the child's unhappy situa-
tion, resolutely made the long and perilous journey, through
dense forests, and over mountains, on horseback and alone,
found him and brought him home, and cared for him as though
he were her own. From her dear lips fell the first words of love
and tenderness he ever knew. Adversity, however, was loth to
quit its prey. At the age of nine he received an accidental blow
from an axe, which made him a cripple for life. Then by a
strange turn of fortune, at thirteen he was turned out into the
world, in midwinter, penniless and almost naked, to care for
himself as best he could. Making his way in his stocking feet
(shoes he had none) to the distant village of Potsdam, he there
served an apprenticeship at the shoe-maker's trade and attained
a proficiency altogether beyond one of his years. Concluding to
try his fortune in the "far west," he set out for the rising village of Rochester, on the Genesee River, his only possessions
consisting of a brave heart, a slender kit of tools, and a pack
of cards, which a friend (?) had generously presented him.
Reaching his place of destination his first business was to bury
the cards, carefully marking the spot so that they might be

found in case of need. He never had occasion to dig them up! Soon after this he fell a victim to the fever-and-ague, and another friend (?) advised the use of ardent spirits as the best and, indeed, the only remedy. Time passed on and he finally awoke to the fact that he had become "a hard drinker." "What!" said he to himself, "Veranus Brownell a slave to whisky; we'll see!" and from that hour not another drop of the foul stuff ever passed his lips. This was in the year 1826. By invitation of a Christian family, and with whom he had been providentially associated, he accompanied them to a camp-meeting held in Canada, and was there soundly converted, and called to the work of the ministry. This was in his 17th year. Up to this time he had never been in school a single day. Feeling the importance of a thorough preparation for his Great Commission, he at once entered upon a systematic course of study. But at the end of his first term at school the authorities of the Church, very unwisely, as he ever afterwards thought, urged him out into the field, under the specious plea, that, while "gaining knowledge is a good thing, saving souls is better." But, notwithstanding his limited advantages, so keen and constant was his thirst for knowledge, so close and accurate were his habits of observation, and, above all, so implicit was his reliance upon the truth of God's Word and the guidance of the Holy Spirit, the embarrassment of his early disadvantages in this direction was ultimately quite overcome. There are multitudes to be found all over the broad field of his public administrations who are ready to testify to the breadth of his learning, the wisdom and maturity of his counsels, and his masterly grasp of the body of revealed truth. On the 19th of November, 1833, he was united in marriage to Miss Margaret Lewis Jenkins, who proved a companion every way worthy of him, fitted both by nature and by grace, to share the trials and responsibilities of his life's great work. Up to the year 1841 his connection had been with the Protestant Methodist Church. But a wider observation led him to the conviction that the thorough system of the Methodist-Episcopal Church gave greater promise of good unto all the people, and he, therefore, with his characteristic promptness of action, still retaining unimpaired the affection and esteem of his former associates in labor, united with the old Genesee Conference at its session held in Dansville in 1841, taking the appointments Hornellsville,

Avoca, Naples, Springwater, Rogersville, Angelica, Conesus
and Sparta. It was while on this last named charge that he
met with the sorest affliction of his life, in the sudden death of
the beloved wife of his youth, December 28, 1852. Her de-
parture left him with ten children, the oldest but seventeen
years of age. Severe as was this bereavement, he was mar-
velously sustained through the trying ordeal. He subsequently
married Miss Lois Showers, a most devoted and confiding companion, who survived him several years. It was at the home of
a Mr. Underhill of Short Tract, N. Y., an uncle of the bride,
that he married his first wife. The young people went to house-
keeping in Messenger's Hollow, a hamlet in the town of Nunda,
Livingston Co., N. Y. They lived here three years, 1833 to
1836. From here they moved to Castile, N. Y., where they
lived until 1841, when Veranus joined the Genesee Conference.
At his death, December 11, 1874, he left 14 children, ten by the
first marriage and four by the second. Nearly all of these, together with the sons-in-law and daughters-in-law, are devoted
members of the Methodist Church and one son, John T., and
two sons-in-law, Rev. Wm. H. Rogers and the Rev. J. B.
Countryman, were members of the Genesee Conference. Were
an explanation of this gratifying result to be sought for, it
would be found in part at least, in the incorruptible integrity
of character which this holy man of God everywhere manifested;
and still more in that warm and attractive piety which glowed
with unvarying luster through all his domestic life, and made
"home" 'the most delightful place in all the world. Moreover,
with him, the Gospel Ministry was not a mere "profession," but
a great and holy calling. It inspired his deepest enthusiasm.
Never through all those years of hard labor and severe ex-
posures, with his "allowance" fixed from year to year at about
starvation point to begin with, and never, but in a solitary in-
stance, fully paid, and with the care of his growing family upon
him, never did one word of complaint fall from his lips within
the hearing of his children. During the several last years of his
life he was afflicted with sciatic rheumatism, which ultimately
became so disabling as to compel him to ask for a superannuated
relation to his conference. This was in the year 1872. Still he
continued to preach nearly every Sabbath, for the most part in
his own neighborhood near Canaseraga, Alleghany Co., N. Y.,
where he was held in the highest veneration, beloved as a father,

and listened to as an Apostle. His last sermon was preached
in September, 1874, just before the Annual Session of the Conference, when, as some of those who were present said, "It
seemed as though an Angel from Heaven had come to declare
the unsearchable riches of Christ." His last days and nights
were passed in the midst of the most excruciating bodily sufferings, but through it all there flowed the same unruffled peace
and cheerful resignation to God's will, for which his whole life
had been remarkable. "It will all be over soon," he would say
with a smile, "and then I shall be at rest." "I have tried not
to flinch at the call of duty, in any manner or place." "But,
oh, I am so unworthy, my only hope is in the infinite atonement
of Christ." To his son and successor in the ministry he said,
"Such visions as I have had on this sick bed, when all alone
with God, such revelations of the glory which shall be. Could
the world behold what I have seen, no soul but would be
charmed to seek after God. Should it please the Lord to raise
me up again, how I will tax this poor tongue to tell the wonders
of His grace." At another time, gazing upon his sons and
daughters, standing in groups around his bed, he said, "The
eight of these affords me infinitely more satisfaction than the
accumulated treasures of the world could give. To know that
my children are walking in the Truth more than repays me for
all the toils and sufferings I have undergone." Then, musing
awhile, he continued, "Often through my earlier ministry, when
it would be proposed by the Authorities of the Church to send
me to this or that appointment, where my children could have
the advantages of school and social cultivation, it would be
objected by the stewards of those places that, "while Brother
Brownell is just the man for the place, and his wife would be
an ornament to any society, yet we cannot think of taking the
burden of supporting such a family of children." None but the
Master knows the heavy weight of sorrow I have borne on this
account." But it is all passed now and I freely give into the
bosom of the Church, what it was so unwilling to help me to
provide for, a band of strong men and women of God, and I
am content." And when at length the hour of his dissolution
was near, when the mists of the dark river had blinded his eyes
to all human sights forever, one of his sons stooped down and
repeated in his ear from the twenty-third Psalm, "Though I
walk through the valley of the shadow of death," at this point

he started, and the words, "No fear! No fear!" burst from his lips, while an unearthly radiance suffused his pallid features, smoothing out the deep lines of pain, and lingering there in indescribable loveliness, until he was laid to his final rest.

It was at the home of a Mr. Underhill, in Short Tract, N. Y., that Veranus Brownell met this gentleman's niece, Miss Margaret Lewis Jenkins. An acquaintance was begun which ripened into love, such love as comes to loyal and trustworthy souls, for he surely was one of Nature's Noblemen, and she was a Perfect Woman, nobly planned. After their marriage, as stated above, they lived for three years at Messenger's Hallow, and then they removed to Castile, N. Y. During this period he worked at his trade and preached, and perpared himself to join the Genesee Conference. During the years of his ministry he continued to work at his trade, for his salaries were never enough to support his family. He purchased a farm in Birdsall and built a house, which came to be known as the Brownell Homestead, and on January 1, 1848, he moved his family there while he preached at Angelica (not very far away). In the fall of 1850, six months after the birth of the tenth child, the Conference ordered them to move to Conesus, and so to Conesus they went. It is a wonder to us today how our Grandmother managed, with such a large family, to move every year, or two. Truly, she must have been a wonderful woman. In 1851 Veranus visited friends and relatives in Pomfret, Vt. He went from Conesus to Chralotte with horse and buggy, his son, John, driving. From there he took a steamer down the lake and river, disembarking at some point nearest to his destination. He returned the same way, John, a lad of 15, making the drive through the forest all the way to Charlotte to meet him. While they lived in Conesus, Margaret's married brother, John Jenkins, and her unmarried brother, Isaac, lived in the Homestead, worked the farm and took care of the place. Previous to this time the rest of the Jenkins family had moved to St. Joseph's Co., Mich. (See Jenkins Family.)

In 1852, Veranus and family wished to return to the Homestead, but as above stated, the house was occupied by John and Isaac Jenkins. So they rented a house for the Winter at Birdsall Center, one mile from the farm, and here on December 18, Margaret gave birth to her eleventh child and both mother and child died. They were buried in the cemetery at Canaserga,

N. Y. As soon as possible the family was moved into the house on the farm, and a young cousin, Jane Brownell, from St. Lawrence Co., N. Y., came to be the head of the household. But she was young and lively and when Veranus would return from the circuit, he frequently found her and the older girls away on pleasure bent, while the younger children were "running wild." Something had to be done at once. So, casting about in his mind for a helpmate, his choice fell upon Margaret's most intimate friend, Lois Showers, of Urbana, N. Y. The great marvel is that she would consider stepping into a house, already full of children, ten in all. But she accepted, and while out on a buggy ride, August 11, 1853, she wearing a new calico dress, and a black silk apron, they decided not to wait longer, and drove to the Methodist parsonage and had the "knot" tied. The following is a more orderly and complete record of the family.

MARGARET LEWIS JENKINS

VERANUS BROWNELL, born March 16, 1810, Pomfret, Vt.; died December 15, 1874, Birdsall, N. Y. Married, November 19, 1833, Short Tract, N. Y., MARGARETT LEWIS JENKINS, born March 18, 1818, Waterloo, N. Y.; died December 18, 1852, Birdsall, N. Y. (See Jenkins Family.) Their children were:

1. JAMES EVAN BROWNELL, born April 18, 1835, died December 19, 1927. Married MELINA COLLER, died March 23, 1909, daughter of JAMES COLLER and CATHERINE GERNERD.

2. JOHN THOMAS BROWNELL, born August 24, 1836, died in Florida, 1886. Married ADELIA SMALLWOOD of Warsaw.

3. ANN MARIA BROWNELL, born 1838, died 1909. Married WILLIAM FLINT.

4. MARTHA ELIZABETH BROWNELL, born July 25, 1840, died June 3, 1914. Married WILLIAM H. ROGERS.

5. HIRAM BROWNELL, born January 22, 1842, ————. Married in 1884 ADELE LARRISON, daughter of WILLIAM LARRISON. Died 1904.

6. MARY JANE BROWNELL, born November 23, 1843, died April 6, 1927. Married ALONZO SLAIGHT, born 1832, died 1904.

7. ELEANOR BROWNELL, born September 20, 1845, died ————. Married REV. J. B. COUNTRYMAN 1865.

8. EMILY BROWNELL, born March 19, 1847, died December 16, 1882. Married GURNEE LARRISON, died 1907.

9. RACHEL LOUISE BROWNELL, born August 23, 1848, died October 14, 1883.

10. ABIGAIL AMANDA BROWNELL, born April 14, 1850, died —— Married EUGENE McNINCH.

11. A child born December 18, 1852. Mother and child died the same day.

The children born to VERANUS BROWNELL and his second wife, LOIS SHOWERS, were:

1. CATHERINE LUCINDA BROWNELL, born June 25, 1855, died ————. Married FRANK TAGGERT BENTLEY August 11, 1887. No issue.

2. JASPER MORSE BROWNELL, born May 25, 1862, died ————. Married GRACE COLTON November 17, 1888.

3. FRANK ELMER BROWNELL, born February 29, 1864, died November 28, 1912. Married GERTRUDE FARNHAM 1879.

4. JOSEPH FLINT BROWNELL, born May 1, 1867, died ————. Married ANNA ROBINSON June 23, 1887.

JAMES EVAN BROWNELL

1. JAMES EVAN BROWNELL, eldest child of VERANUS and MARGARET (JENKINS) BROWNELL, was born in Messenger's Hollow, Liv. Co., N. Y., April 18, 1835. His early childhood was spent in different places as his father moved according to custom of Methodist itinerants in those days. The places were: Castile, Hornellsville, Avoca, Naples, South Dansville and Birdsall, Angelica and Conesus. While here James secured a position to "clerk" in a store (called Dart's Store) and he remained here when the family moved for the second time to Birdsall. When he was twenty-five years old, November 22, 1860, he married MALINA BRADNER COLLER, daughter of JAMES and CATHERINE (GERNERD) COLLER. She was born May 12, 1838, in Scottsburg, Liv. Co., N. Y., and died March 23, 1909, in Rochester, N. Y. For his entire life James E. Brownell was engaged in the mercantile business.

Before his marriage, he had formed a partnership with Alonzo T. Slaight, who afterwards became his brother-in-law, and they kept a General Store in Scottsburg, N. Y. The firm of Slaight and Brownell was known far and near as a reliable, trustworthy firm, and for many years they did a flourishing business. In the year 1894 they sold the business in Scottsburg to Mr. Chas. A. Bateman, and both families moved to Rochester.

A. T. Slaight engaged in the Wholesale Dental Goods business, with rooms in the Power's Bldg., and James Brownell conducted a store similar to the one in Scottsburg in Lyell Ave., the firm name remaining the same, Slaight and Brownell, Mr. Slaight being a silent partner. He continued in this business with his son, John Laverne, for many years.

In the year 1911 he retired from active work, at the age of 76 years, and the following year went to make his home with his daughter, Mrs. Walter Dryer. Mr. Brownell lived to the great age of 92 years, and died peacefully while asleep in bed. the date of his demise was December 19, 1927. His children were:

1. FLORA E. BROWNELL, born in Scottsburg, January 24, 1862. Her childhood was spent in the place of her birth. In 1879 she went to Genesee Wesleyan Seminary at Lima, N. Y., where she and ADELE LARRISON were room-mates, and where Adele graduated. Flora's mother being very ill, she was taken to a Sanatorium for treatment, and the home needing a head, Flora was unable to return to the Seminary for the final term ,and so did not graduate. Afterward

ADELE LARRISON married HIRAM BROWNELL, brother of JAMES EVAN, and so became Flora's aunt, altho there was not much difference in their ages. On December 31, 1885, Flora married OTIS WALTER DRYER of Rush, N. Y., son of ORRIN CARPENTRER and ADALINE SOPHRONIA (STULL) DRYER. They have made their home in the city of Rochester, where Mr. Dryer has been one of the best known architects for many years. Their home is on East Ave., corner of Penfield Rd.

Their children are:

a. HARWOOD BROWNELL DRYER, born May 19, 1895. Harwood attended the Rochester schools, graduating from East High School January, 1914. Planning to enter partnership with his father after due preparation he took up practical work in his father's office for two years, and then went to Cornell University, where he took a Special Course in Architecture. In 1918, when he left school, there was a strong call for college men in the Ship Industry at Bethlehem, Penna., it being war time and ships so greatly needed. So after spending one week-end at home he went to Bethlehem, where he remained until December after the Armistice was signed. He is in partnership with his father with offices at 315 Alexander St. Is unmarried and lives at the homestead.

b. ELEANOR ONNOLEE DRYER, born April 20, 1899. She graduated from East High School in June, 1917, was married May 19, 1923, to LEIGH MASON FITCH, son of FRANK E. and HATTIE (WESTCOTT) FITCH, of Rochester, N. Y. He spent one year during the World War "Somewhere in France." Is now a contractor and builder, and resides on the Penfield Rd.
Their children are:

  1. *Mason Brownell Fitch,* born September 26, 1925.
  2. *Robert Leigh Fitch,* born August 9, 1928.

2. JOHN LAVERNE BROWNELL, born in Scottsburg, N. Y., December 18, 1863. Unmarried. Resides at 963 Plymouth Ave. N., Rochester, N. Y. He has been a merchant all his life. At first working for his father in Scottsburg, then for seventeen years in the Lyell Ave. store. During late years he has filled a responsible position in Sibley's Department Store.

3. ONNOLEE BROWNELL, born in Scottsburg, N. Y., August 23, 1868. Attended the public school in Scottsburg and later Genesee Wesleyan Seminary at Lima, N. Y. Was married July 14, 1892, to SAMUEL EDGAR PATTERSON, born July 24, 1860. Their home is at 963 Plymouth Ave. N., Rochester, N. Y. He has been for some years with the North East Alliance Corporation. They have one child.

a. FLORENCE MARGUERITE PATTERSON, born January 15, 1895, was
   graduated from West High School in January, 1914, and married April 6, 1920, to GEORGE ALVIN JOHNSON of Long Beach,
   Cal., born July 30, 1893. He graduated from Ohio State University in Electrical Engineering. He served in the U. S. Army
   during the World War. Since that time has been employed in
   several responsible positions by the North East Appliance Corporation. At present is at the head of the Service Department.
   They reside at 1200 Lake Ave., Rochester, N. Y.
   No children.

JOHN THOMAS BROWNELL

II. JOHN THOMAS BROWNELL, second child of Veranus Brownell and Margaret (Jenkins) Brownell, was born in Castile, N. Y., August 24, 1836, and died in Tangerine, Florida, May 26, 1886. He was converted in early life at a camp meeting held at Grove, N. Y. He took his preparatory course at Rogersville Academy, of which at that time Rev. Isaiah McMahon was principal. He entered Genesee College at Lima, N. Y., in 1859, and graduated in 1863 with the highest honors. During the next two years he taught in a seminary at Kent's Hill, Maine. He was married in Ripley, N. Y., to MISS ADELIA SMALLWOOD, a lady of superior gifts of mind and heart, also a graduated of Genesee College of Lima, N. Y. Though eminently successful as a teacher, he was actuated by a conviction that the ministry was to be his life's work, and, consequently, he joined the East Genesee Conference of the Methodist Episcopal Church in the Fall of 1865 and from that time on he continued to preach serving as appointed the following churches: Tonawanda, Naples, Bath, Lima, Warsaw, Geneseo, Lyons, Mansfield and Auburn. It was while in his first year in Auburn that he met the great loss of his life—the death of his beloved wife. No two were ever more happily and completely united in matrimony that they. And it was consequently a great strain on him to go on alone in the work of the ministry. Still he toiled barvely on until forced by failing strength to resign his work, greatly to the regret of his church. It was while seeking health and strength in the sunny clime of Florida that the end came. The children which had come to bless this so early sundered home were:

1. JOHN VERANUS BROWNELL, born June 18, 1868, and died February 6, 1898. He was a most remarkable young man. After the death of his parents he made his home with his uncle and aunt, MR. GEORGE K. and MRS. EMMA (SMALLWOOD) POWELL, of Wilkes-Barre, Pa, graduating with high honors from the schools of that city, he entered Syracuse University in 1887 and graduated in 1891, receiving the degree of A.B. In 1894 the University conferred upon him the A.M. degree. He studied law in Wilkes-Barre, Pa., from 1891 to 1894, and was admitted to the bar in 1894. He specialized in railroad law, and went to Los Angeles, Cal., to begin his practice. But death cut his career short and he went to join his parents in the life beyond.

2. MARGARET BROWNELL, born August 15, 1874, and died in California in 1925. She was but five years old when her parents died, at which

time she came to make her home with her uncle, WILLIAM H. ROGERS, and aunt, MARTHA ELIZABETH (BROWNELL) ROGERS. She graduated at Genesee Wesleyan Semininary, Lima, N. Y., and Woman's College, Baltimore, Md., 1896, receiving the degree of A. B. Two years later she married LEWIS S. POWELL, son of GEORGE K. and EMMA (SMALLWOOD) POWELL, of Wilkes-Barre, Pa. They were married in Canoga, N. Y., by REV. WILLIAM H. ROGERS and went to California to make their home in Los Angeles. They had the following children:

a. JOHN POWELL, born 1899, died 1917.

b. GEORGE POWELL, born 1903. Married 1923, RITA PUTNAM.. One child.

c. LEWIS THORNTON POWELL, born, 1913. In high school, Fallbrook, Cal., 1926.

d. KENNETH POWELL.. No record.

e. CHARLES POWELL born, 1917. In grammar school, Fallbrook, 1926..

Ann Maria Brownell Flint

III. ANN MARIA BROWNELL, third child of Veranus Brownell
and Margaret Lewis (Jenkins) Brownell, was born in Castile,
Wyo. Co., N. Y., May 12, 1838, and died in Kanona, N. Y.,
November 6, 1910. Her childhood was spent in the Brownell
Homestead at Birdsall, N. Y. She married, December 13, 1854,
William Lewis Flint, who was born in South Dansville, July 20,
1836, and died December 13, 1903, in his home near Gas
Springs, N. Y. He was the son of Joseph Flint, born January 9,
1811, in Onondaga Co., N. Y., and Susan Philips, born 1809;
died 1851; married 1835. They lived on Oak Hill, town of
South Dansville, N. Y. William Flint served two years in the
Civil War and was honorably discharged. With broken health,
he came home from the war and spent the remainder of his
life on his farm. Their children were:

1. JAMES NELSON FLINT, born October 25, 1856, Burns, N. Y. Married
December 25, 1893, FLORA EMERY, born March 2, 1866, daughter of
ASHBEL EMERY and MARY COLLINS of Hornell, N. Y. They had
one daughter, viz:

   a. LELA MAY FLINT, born April 21, 1896. She married August 1,
   1919, ROY KELLEY, born July 23, 1896, son of MYRON and
   LEONA (OSBORN) KELLEY, of Freemont,, N. Y.

   They have one son,

      1. *Dean Kelley*, born December 16, 1923.

2. GEORGE WALTER FLINT, born February, 28, 1859. He was twice married, first, November 27, 1877, married HATTIE DAVIS, daughter of
WILLIAM DAVIS and CORILLA WHITFORD, born ———, died February 28, 1897; ROSIE MYRTLE WARREN, born ———, died June
12, 1898. She was the daughter of JAMES WARREN and MELINDA
(CARNES) WARREN. Children by the first wife:

   a. FREDERICK LAVERNE FLINT, born March 26, 1899, and died February 18, 1927. Married August 26, 1903, GRACE GATES, born
   ———, daughter of JOHN E. GATES *and* EMMA ALICE
   PARKS. They live in Hornell, N. Y. They have one son,

      1. *Kenneth Flint* born January 12, 1909.

   b. JAMES WALTER FLINT, born April 1, 1885, died September 25, 1892.
   Child by second wife.

   c. CLARENCE GEORGE FLINT, born June 5, 1898, died two days later,
   and the mother died one week later.

3. ELIZABETH LUNA FLINT, born March 19, 1861. She married twice,
first May 10, 1876, RICHARD WOODARD. (Divorced.) Second, No-

vember 17, 1882, as his second wife, DEWITT C. DIMMICK, son of
DR. MARLIN D. DIMMICK and ROSE ANN BENNETT, of Canandaigua.

4. JENNIE AMANDA FLINT, born July 23, 1866. Married April 26, 1886,
CHARLES HENRY WARREN, born August 19, 1862, died ————. He
was the son of JAMES and MELINDA (CARNES) WARREN of Sparta,
N. Y. Their children are:

a. MYRTLE ANN WARREN, born March 7, 1887. Married April 28,
1908, JACOB H. SNYDER, of Sodus, N. Y., born May 14, 1883,
son of ELMER and LUCY (WOOD) SNYDER. Their children are:

1. *Howard Lincoln Snyder*, born February 12, 1909.
2. *Una Margaret Snyder*, born September 25, 1910.
3. *Donna Elinor Snyder*, born March 28, 1913.
4. *Edna Eloise Snyder*, born October 25, 1914.
5. *Marjorie Elna Snyder*, born October 6, 1916.
6. *Roger Dudley Snyder*, born November 27, 1918.
7. *Dorothy Vera Snyder*, born April 12, 1920.

b. ARDEN LEWIS WARREN, of Burns, N. Y., born May 14, 1892.
Married February 1, 1926, VIOLET DEY, born April 26, 1907,
daughter of LAMONT and QUEEN (TERWILLIGER) DEY. Their
children are:

1. *Beulah Violet Warren*, born November 1927.
2. *Nelson Lewis Warren* born October 9 1928.

c. JAMES LESTER WARREN, born November 28, 1895. Lives
with his mother in Canaseraga, N. Y.

d. MARGUERITE ELIZABETH WARREN, born January 14, 1898. Married August 25, 1915, EMMET ROBERT KEOUGH, born February
7, 1888, son of PATRICK and MARGARET (KING) KEOUGH of
Whitney's Crossing, N. Y. Their children are:

1. *Robert Lewis Keough,* born January 15, 1917.
2. *James Thomas Keough,* born September 22, 1918.
3. *Herbert Francis Keough,* born August 11, 1920.
4. *Kenneth Laverne Keough,* born November 1, 1922.
5. *Myrtle Agnes Keough,* born April 8, 1926.
6. *Harry Eugene Keough,* born September 2, 1928.

5. HERBERT FLINT, born April 27, 1869, died March 21, 1870.

6. EDWIN CLIFTON FLINT, born March 28, 1871, died October 22, 1916.
Married ————, EMMA J. BROWN, born ————, died January
22, 1917, daughter of WILLIAM and MARY (RAWLINS) BROWN of
Gas Springs, N. Y. They made their home in Gas Springs. Here
Mr. and Mrs. Edwin C. Flint spent their married life. He was a
great sufferer from rheumatism, but was patient and uncomplaining.
He was universally respected not only for his fortitude in suffering,
but also for his interest in the welfare of others. His widow and
son continue to make their home in Gas Springs.

a. LELAND BROWN FLINT, born May 22, 1901.

7. JOSEPH BENSON FLINT, born December 10, 1872. He was twice married, first June 11, 1917, BEATRICE SUSAN BURRIS, born ————, died January 20, 1919, daughter of STEPHEN BURRIS and SUSAN (FISHER), and second, October 25, 1919, CORA ADELLA LUTHER, born ————, daughter of ARBA P. LUTHER and MAE (TROWBRIDGE) LUTHER. There were no children by the first wife. By the second wife the following were born:

a. MAY BELLE ANNA FLINT, born June 27, 1920.

b. FLORA HENRIETTA FLINT, born January 2, 1922.

c. MARION WILLIAM FLINT, born September 22, 1924.

d. DANIEL JOSEPH FLINT, born July 4, 1928.

8. MARGARET MARIA FLINT, born October 25, 1874, died January 9, 1895. Married ————, WESLEY WILLIAM MAYDOLE, born ————, son of DYER MAYDOLE and ANN (————) MAYDOLE. They lived in Klipnockey, a community near Gas Springs, N. Y. They had one child:

a. VERANUS MAYDOLE, born January 4, 1895, and died about three months later

Martha Elizabeth Brownell Rogers

IV. MARTHA ELIZABETH BROWNELL was born in Castile, N. Y., July 25, 1840, and died in Lucerne Valley, California, June 3, 1914. She married, July 3, 1861, in Troupsburg, N. Y., Rev. Wm. H. Rogers, Principal of Troupsburg Academy, and where she had been teaching during that school year. Rev. David Nutten, the Presiding Elder of Hornellsville District of the East Genesee Conference, performed the ceremony, before the student body as a surprise, closing number on the Commencement Program. William Henry Rogers was born October 21, 1834, in Willing, Alleghany Co., N. Y., son of Charles and Lucy (Chandler) Rogers. He graduated in 1859 from Alfred University as also did Martha Elizabeth Brownell. For a few years they both followed the teaching profession and he had a regular appointment to preach also. For nearly 40 years he carried on the double work of teaching during the week and preaching on Sundays. After graduating from Alfred University he took a post-graduate course at Genesee College, Lima, N. Y., graduating with the degree of Master of Arts in 1861. He joined the Methodist East Genesee Conference in the Fall of that year and the rest of his life was spent as stated above. He was Chaplain of the 189th Reg't, New York Volunteers, in the Civil War, serving from the raising of the regiment to the close of the war. He died December 20, 1915, in Los Angeles, Calif. They are buried side by side in the beautiful cemetery of that city. Their children were:

1. JOHN BROWNELL ROGERS, born in Greenwood, N. Y., April 21, 1863. Married July 8, 1891, VESTA OLIVIA CLAIR of Willing, Allegany County, N. Y. Ceremony performed by REV. W. H. ROGERS. She was the daughter of DAVID S. and EMMA (ELSTER) CLAIR. VESTA O. CLAIR was born March 4, 1871, in Whitestown ,N. Y. J. BROWNELL ROGERS was a graduate of Syracuse University (1889). Taught school for three years and then in the year 1892 joined the Central New York Conference and began preaching. After several years in the ministry he took a position with the Pyrrhocide Clinic of New York City and has since been conducting an Educational Bureau for the Prevention of Pyorrhea, from his residence in Freeville, N. Y. Children:

    a. DANA CLAIR ROGERS, born June 4, 1892, Erie, Pa. Married April 15, 1915, LOLA MAY HUNT, born January 9, 1896, Albion, Washington. They were married in Los Molines Calif. Present address Artois, Calif., where he is Station Agent, Southern Pacific Railroad. DANA CLAIR ROGERS has been engaged in railroad work all his life. Children:

1. *William Clair Rogers,* born March 26, 1916, Biggs, Cal.
2. *Vesta Lucile Rogers,* born October 15, 1918, Fair Ooaks, Cal.;
   died January 4, 1919, Freeville, N. Y.
3. *John Brownell Rogers,* born December 22, 1919, New York City.
4. *Evelyn Jane Rogers,* born September 5, 1921, Los Molines, Cal.
5. *Betty June Rogers,* born June 13, 1925, Orland, Cal.

b. VERNER BROWNELL ROGERS, born July 18, 1894, Conquest, N. Y.
Married February 5, 1916, ANNA E. WILLARD, born August 21,
1887, in Freeville, N. Y. He has been engaged in railroad work
since leaving school and is at present Train Dispatcher Hudson
Division, New York Central R. R. Address 2213 Turnbull Ave.,
New York City. Children:

1. *Willard Brownell Rogers,* born November 25, 1928, New York
   City.
2. *Donald Delos Rogers,* born March 8, 1920, New York City.
3. *Franklin Robert Rogers,* born July 25, 1921, New York City.

c. DAVID DELOS ROGERS, born September 18, 1898, Freeville, N. Y.
Married November 16, 1922, HELEN MAY MATSON, born August
11, 1902, Binghamton, N. Y. DAVID DELOS ROGERS is clerk
in Claim Agent's Office New York Central Freight Office, Syracuse, N. Y. Child:

1. *Enid Clair Rogers,* born January 31, 1928.

d. HELEN ELIZABETH ROGERS, born August 8, 1900, Freeville, N. Y.
She is a Captain in the Salvation Army, having been sometime
stationed in Pittsburgh, Pa., but now is filling a ten year appointment in Buenos Aires, Argentina. South America, having
now completed about one-half of the ten year term. She is
not married.

e. EDITH ONNOLEE ROGERS, born April 19, 1905, Van Etten, N. Y.
Married, October 28, 1924, in Eastwood. N. Y., EARNEST M.
BAJUS, born July 7 1905 in Fayetteville. N. Y. They make
their home in Syracuse, N. Y., where he is employed in the
Crouse-Hines Mfg. Co. Their address is 263 Wayland Road.
Syracuse, N. Y. They have two children:

1. *John Clair Bajus,* born May 27, 1926.
2. *Kenyon Brownell Bajus,* born November 8, 1928.

f. ALICE MARION ROGERS, twin of the above EDITH ONNOLEE, lived
only a few days.

2 LOWELL LINCOLN ROGERS, born in Willing, Allegheny County. N. Y.,
May 14. 1865. Married February 22, 1893, JESSIE RUTH COE,
of Syracuse, N. Y. She was the daughter of JEROME H. COE, M. D.,
and his first wife, FRANCES ELIZABETH HUNTINGTON. They lived in
Oswego, N. Y., at the time of her birth, which was January 27,
1868. She died in Medina. N. Y., September 27, 1927. LOWELL
LINCOLN ROGERS graduated from Syracuse University in 1889. After

teaching for three years he joined the Genesee Conference of the Methodist Church in 1892 and has been preaching ever since. From 1913 to 1919 he was Superintendent of Corning District. Children:

a. RUTH COE ROGERS, born in Youngstown, N. Y., November 23, 1893. Graduated from Syracuse University, 1918. Taught art in the Schools of Canastota for four years. Married September 21, 1922, WILLIAM A. FRANCHELL of Canastota, N. Y., born November 1, 1898, in Hazelton, Pa., son of VINCENZO FRANCH-ELL, born January 17, 1856, in Provinca-Consence-Town Paterno, Italy, and his wife, VINCENZA STUMPA, born November 6, 1861, died October 1, 1918, born in Provinca-Consence-town Cuti, and died in Canastota, N. Y. One year later they moved to Medina, N. Y., where MR. FRANCHELL engaged in the mercantile business. Their address is 310 Park Ave., Medina, N. Y. Children:

> 1. *William Rogers Franchell*, born in Oneida (hospital), August 22, 1923.
> 2. *Jerome Coe Franchell*, born in Medina, N. Y., March 17, 1927.

b. VINCENT JEROME ROGERS, born at North Ridge, N. Y., September 17, 1896. Graduated from Syracuse University 1920. Completion of his college course was delayed two years because of time spent in the World War. Married September 1, 1921, RUTH E. TOLSON of Shawnee-on-Delaware, Pa., where her father, HENRY W. TOLSON, was pastor of the Presbyterian Church. Her mother was EVA DAVIS WARREN. He performed the ceremony, assisted by the father of the groom. MR. VINCENT J. ROGERS is a Y. M. C. A. Secretary of Buffalo, N. Y. His address, Y. M. C. A. Building, N. Delaware, corner of Avery Ave., Buffalo, N. Y. One child:

> 1. *Vincent Jerome Rogers, Jr.*, born June 1, 1922.

c. HERBERT BROWNELL ROGERS, born in Rochester, N. Y., May 19, 1903. Graduated from Syracuse University 1925. Married July 28, 1928, EVA MAE BARKER, a graduate nurse, Highland Hospital, Rochester, N. Y., daughter of ERNEST and ALIDA (THOMPSON) BARKER or Nunda N. Y. HERBERT B. ROGERS is Executive Secretary of the Lawrenceville Branch of the Y. M. C. A. of Pittsburgh, Pa. Mr. and Mrs. Rogers were married in Medina, N. Y., the father of the groom performing the ceremony. Their address is 1224 Trevanion St., Pittsburgh, Pa. They have one child,

> 1. *Herbert Rogers, Jr.*, born April 30, 1930.

d. LOWELL LINCOLN ROGERS, JR., born in Silver Springs, N. Y., February 11, 1907. Spent four years in the High School at Medina, N. Y., and took a technical course in Syracuse. He is now Traveling Salesman for the Graves Elevator Works in Rochester, N. Y.

3. GRACE EVANGELINE ROGERS, born in Springville, N. Y., in 1870, and died 1872.

4. WILLIAM CLAIRE ROGERS of St. Louis, Mo., 5463 Delmar Ave., born in East Ashford, N. Y., June 23, 1874. Graduated from Syracuse University 1909 and of University of the State of New York 1916, A. M. He is a Veteran of the Spanish War, Co. C, 3d N. Y. Vol. Inf. World War Major, Ordnance Dept., U. S. Army. Lt.-Col., Ordnance Dept., U. S. Army Reserve. Served the country as Commissioner of Labor during the World War. Was for several years Supt. of the Board of Charities of New York State and Chairman of the Board of Mediation and Arbitration of New York. He married August 22 1900, ELMA MASTEN, born August 22, 1876, of Genoa, N. Y., graduate of Cornell University 1900 B. S., daughter of ALFRED AVERY and ANN MARIA (ROBINSON) MASTEN. The ceremony was performed by REV. L. L. ROGERS, brother of the groom. They had one child, a daughter:

  a. ELIZABETH ANN ROGERS, born March 29, 1902, in Freeville, N. Y., and died July 2, 1910, in Albany, N. Y., and her body was laid to rest in the cemetery in Genoa, N. Y.

5. ROBERT ROGERS born 1877, in East Palmyra, N. Y. Lived only five days.

6. FLORENCE BELL ROGERS, born 1880, in Dundee, N. Y., died 1881.

HIRAM BROWNELL

V. HIRAM BROWNELL, fifth child of Veranus and Margaret
Jenkins Brownell, born in Hornell(then Hornellsville), N. Y.,
January 22, 1842. At the outbreak of the Civil War, Hiram en-
listed in the 13th Infantry of New York Volunteers. He was
attached to the Army of the Potomac and took part in many of
the major engagements of the war, including the Peninsular
Campaign and the Seven Days' Battle, the second battle of
Bull Run, Antietam and Fredericksburg. In the last named battle he was seriously wounded in the left hip by a bursting shell.
He was left on the battlefield as dead, and in fact did nearly
die from the loss of blood. All the remainder of his life he has
suffered from the effects of this wound. At the expiration of
his term of enlistment he was honorably discharged from the
army and returned home for a short period of rest. Then he
went west to Kansas and New Mexico, at that time a wild, un-
settled country. He engaged in hotel work, then railroad con-
struction on the new Santa Fe Lines, cattle raising and general
farming, at one time owning a farm on the site of which the
city of Great Bend, Kansas, was afterward built. A series of
disasters common in the lives of those early pioneers overtook
his ranching efforts—grasshoppers, droughts and tornadoes.
Broken financially and discouraged over the repeated failures,
he returned east in 1882, after 20 years' absence. While on a
visit to the home of his sister, Emily, wife of Gurnee Larrison,
near Westfield, Penn., he met and in 1884 married Adele Larrison, daughter of William Larrison (brother of Gurnee) and
Susan Pemberton Larrison. They had the following named
children:

1. HENRY LARRISON BROWNELL, born April 9, 1885. Married EVA BUR-
   RITT of Dubois, Pa. Henry is a railroader, having been constantly
   employed by the Buffalo and Susquehanna R. R. since 1900.

2. JAMES VERANUS BROWNELL, born July 25, 1887. Married MARIE
   MYERS of Williamsport, daughter of WILLIAM and LOUISE (KELLEAR)
   MYERS. They live in Washington, D. C., and have two children:
       1. *James Franklin Brownell*, born December 23, 1917.
       2. *Robert William Brownell*, born March 16, 1919.

3. ROBERT BROWNELL, born July 27, 1891. Married ELIZABETH BANKS,
   daughter of JAMES and ALICE (CARROLL) BANKS. They live in
   Washington, D. C., and have no chlidren.

MARY JANE BROWNELL SLAIGHT

VI. MARY JANE BROWNELL, sixth child of VERANUS and
MARGARET (JENKINS) BROWNELL, was born in Naples,
N. Y., November 27, 1843. Her childhood was sepnt in South
South Dansville, Birdsall, Angelica, Conesus, then Birdsall
again, due to the frequent moving as was the custom of the
Methodist Itinerancy. From Birdsall, Jennie (as she was
called) taught country schools, then attended the Springville
Academy, and later became a teacher there, under her brother-
in-law, William H. Rogers, the Principal. She was married there
on the closing day of school, June 23, 1870, to ALONZO TRU-
MAN SLAIGHT, who was then in partnership with her brother,
James, in general merchandise business in Scottsburg, New
York. He was born in Scottsburg, May 10, 1833, and died in
Rochester, N. Y., February 19, 1904. They lived in Scottsburg for several years, where three children were born. (See
record below.) In 1878, with proper provision for the care of
the children, Jennie entered the Medical Department of the
University of Buffalo, to obtain the degree of M. D. She was
graduated in 1880 and was a pioneer among woman physicians.
That year her husband sold out his partnership in Scottsburg
and moved the family to Rochester, N. Y., where he had arranged a partnership with Charles A. Davis in the dental supply business under the name of Davis & Co., and Jennie in
the practice of medicine. She became a friend of Susan
Brownell Anthony, Sarah A. Dolly and other women interested
in the welfare of the so-called weaker sex, and through their
efforts the Rochester Free Dispensary for Women was organ-
ized and conducted by women in the interest of the poor wom-
en of the city. Dr. Slaight was appointed to and accepted the
position of the first woman city physician in Rochester, and attended women in hovels day and night as medical attention was
required, for the merely nominal salary of three hundred dol-
lars per year. This work, together with the services given the
Free Dispensary, left little time to devote to private practice,
but such unselfish devotion to the welfare of those less for-
tunate prevailed throughout her life. After her husband's
death in 1904, she discontinued the practice of medicine, but
retained her association with women's organizations. She was
a member of the First Methodist Church of Rochester until
removing to Rye, N. Y., in 1924, after which she attended the
Methodist Church of that town. She died in the family home

at Rye, N. Y., April 6, 1927. After A. T. Slaight's retirement from the Dental Supply business, he entered into partnership with T. D. Snyder under the firm name of Slaight & Snyder, Real Estate, and continued to give his attention to this business until his death. Their life together was a true example of ideal family devotion and unselfish love. Their bodies are laid to rest side by side in the family plot in Mt. Hope Cemetery in Rochester, N. Y. The following is the record of their children:

1. HERBERT ALONZO SLAIGHT was born in Scottsburg, N. Y., July 23, 1871. He attended the public schools in Rochester, Genesee Wesleyan Seminary, and Rochester University, graduating in the Class of 1893. He was a member of the Delta Psi Fraternity. He engaged in the dental supply business, organizing the firm of Parkington & Slaight of Albany and New York City, and later consolidated with the Cleveland Dental Mfg. Co., becoming its President. He was also Treasurer of the Dentinol and Pyrozide Co. After retiring from active association with the Cleveland Dental Mfg. Co., he became President of the Childent Company. He was a member of the Masonic Lodge in Albany, N. Y. On June 28, 1899, he married MISS HARRIETTE HAMILTON, born November 29, 1878, in Castile, N. Y., daughter of EDWARD and FRANCES (BURCH) HAMILTON, of Perry, N. Y. Their children are:

    a. HAMILTON TRUMAN SLAIGHT, born in New York City, November 1, 1905, graduating from Kenyon College and the Harvard Graduate School of Business Administration. He engaged in the Banking Business in 1928 in New York City.

    b. JANE BROWNELL SLAIGHT, born in Cleveland, Ohio, June 30, 1915.

2. MARY LULU SLAIGHT, second child of ALONZO and MARY JANE (BROWNELL) SLAIGHT, was born in Scottsburg, N. Y., March 11, 1873. She attended the public schools of Rochester Genesee Wesleyan Seminary at Lima, N. Y., and the Livingston Park Seminary of Rochester. On February 24, 1897, she was married in Rochester to JOHN ABRAM HANSON, born in Rushford, Minn., February 12, 1869, son of ABRAM K. HANSON and his wife, ELIZABETH DAVIS, who respectively came to this country from Norway and Wales and were married in Watertown, Wis., June 29, 1857.

    a. LELAND SLAIGHT HANSON, only child of JOHN and LULU HANSON, was born in Rochester, N. Y., July 18, 1898. He attended the public schools of that city and graduated from St. John's Military Academy at Manlius, N. Y. Enlisted in the U. S. Army and was stationed in the Officers' Training Camp in Virginia. Following the World War, he gained experience, both in production and selling and became associated with the Chase

Brass & Copper Co. of New York City. On April 9, 1927, he married LEILA MORANGE, only surviving daughter of EDWARD AUSTIN and JULIA ANNE (SOWERSBY) MORANGE, born in New York City, October 7, 1903. One child:

    1. *Leila Morange Hanson,* born December 25, 1929.

3. LELAND VERANUS SLAIGHT, youngest child of ALONZO *and* MARY JANE (BROWNELL) SLAIGHT, was born in Scottsburg, N. Y., February 24, 1876. He attended the Public schools of Rochester and entered the University of Rochester in 1893. He united with the Delta Psi Fraternity. Spent some time in the study of law and later conducted Slaight's Real Estate Exchange in Rochester. In 1908 he became the President of the Dentinol & Pyrozide Co. of New York City, but maintained his home and real estate interests in Rochester. until 1924, when the home was established in Rye, N. Y. Here he became President of the Long View Heights Development Co., and a Director of the Rye Operating Co., and the Whitby Holding Corporation. He is a life member of the Masonic order and Elks. in Rochester, N. Y. He is unmarried.

ELEANOR BROWNELL COUNTRYMAN

VII. ELEANOR BROWNELL, born in Naples, N. Y., September
20, 1845. While attending school at Troupsburg Academy,
Troupsburg, N. Y., she met and afterward married REV. J.
BENSON COUNTRYMAN of the East Genesee Conference
of the Methodist Episcopal Church. He was son of JOHN A.
I. COUNTRYMAN and MEGDALENA SNYDER of Men-
don, N. Y., born April 13, 1840. He began his life's work in
the ministry in 1864 and continued for 44 years, only missing
one Sunday's duties in all that time from ill health. He retired from active service a few years before his death, which
took place June 28, 1927, in Williamson, N. Y., where they
were then living. Their children were:

1. EVERETT CLAYTON COUNTRYMAN, born May 23, 1867, in East Otto,
   N. Y. After attending Cazenovia and Lima Seminaries, he entered
   Syracuse University, graduating in 1889. He was a member of the
   Psi Upsilon Fraternity. He studied law and was admitted to the
   Bar in New York State. For eight years he edited the "Gowanda
   Leader," and during that time he acquired his Ph. D. degree from
   Taylor University. He is now accountant in the Department of
   Mental Hygiene in the State Capitol, Albany, N. Y. He married
   (first) July 21, 1897, ANNAH M. SHERMAN, of Gowanda, N. Y. She
   died in Albany, N. Y. August 21 1911. He married (second) August
   12, 1912, ELLA M. FERGUSON of Waverly, Ohio, daughter of SAM-
   UEL FERGUSON and JOSEPHINE CLEMONS of Waverly.

2. EDITH FLORENCE COUNTRYMAN, born May 23, 1867, twin of EVERETT
   CLAYTON COUNTRYMAN. She attended Syracuse University, College of Fine Arts, graduating in the class of 1889. She was a member
   of the Kappa Alpha Theta Sorority. She married August 16, 1898,
   REV. PHILIP HEDRICK of the Genesee Conference, Methodist Episcopal Church. Their married life together was short, for she passed
   away December 20, 1898. She had a beautiful character, was pure
   in soul, high-minded in life, and of an exceptional artistic tempera-
   ment, leaving behind her many examples of her skill in oil paint-
   ings and other works of art.

3. MARY ONNOLEE COUNTRYMAN was born May 7, 1877. She attended
   Goucher College, Baltimore, Md. Was a member of the Kappa
   Alpha Theta Sorority. She graduated in 1899. She married June
   29, 1910, HERBERT EDGAR SPERRY, M. D., of Rochester, N. Y., son
   of BURTON E. SPERRY and MARY VINTON of Rochester N. Y. He
   was a graduate of the Medical College of Union University. In 1914,
   he took post graduate work in New York City. During the World
   War he was commissioned Captain and stationed at Camp Gordon
   Base Hospital. They are now residing in Williamson, N. Y.

EMMA BROWNELL LARRISON

VIII. EMILY BROWNELL, born in South Dansville, N. Y.,
March 10, 1847, and died on the home farm south of Westfield,
Pa., December 16, 1882. She married, May 14, 1865, Gurnee
Larrison of Westfield, Pa., born November 17, 1826, and died
March 30, 1907, son of William and Sarah (Stryker) Larrison.
Their children were:

1. HARRY HALE LARRISON, born May 7, 1866, ————. He married,
August 26, 1891, EVA DOUGLASS, born October 18, 1871, daughter of
JOHN and NANCY (LABAR) DOUGLASS. They have made their home
in Sabinville, Pa. Their children are:

a. EVERETT DOUGLASS LARRISON, born September 26, 1892. Married IVA KILBORN, April 14, 1914, daughter of JOHN and ENSIE
(SCHOONOVER) KILBORN. She was born April 14, 1893. One child:

1. *Wendall Larrison*, born May 13, 1918.

b. HELEN MABLE LARRISON, born December 14, 1893. She married,
September 16, 1911, LYNN SHERMAN YALE, born December 4,
1892, son of JAY and MINNIE (PARSHALL) YALE. One child:

1. *Jack Alden Yale*, born April 17, 1923.

c. JAY GURNEE LARRISON, born October 10, 1895. He married, October 9, 1928, MADELINE BUMP, born August 20, 1909, daughter
of NORMAN and EDNA (CHILSON) BUMP.

d. EMILY ELAINE LARRISON, born March 31, 1901. She married,
November 27, 1917, MILFORD HAMILTON STEBBINS, son of GEORGE
and ALTA (SMITH) STEBBINS, born March 28, 1896. Their
children are:

1. *Evaline Alta Stebbins*, born June 22, 1919.
2. *Milford Junior Stebbins*, born March 27, 1924.
3. *Monolee A. Stebbins*, born January 25, 1926.
4. *Beverly Joan Stebbins*, born August 20, 1929.

e. ELSIE JANE LARRISON, born September 19, 1908. She married,
May 18, 1929, FRANK CAULKINS, son of NELSON ADELBERT and
JESSIE BLANCH (THATCHER) CAULKINS. He was born Decem-
ber 15, 1905.

f. GILBERT REED LARRISON, born December 10, 1911.

2. MARION LOUISE LARRISON, born ————, 1867, ————. Married,
————, 1893, JAMES SEAGER, born, 1861, son of _____
and _____. They live in Westfield, Pa. Their
children are:

a. MARGARET SEAGER _____.

b. ONNOLEE SEAGER --.

3. JAMES ROY LARRISON, born January 31, 1871. He married, April 15,
1893, EUNICE HANES, daughter of JEROME and EMMA (PRITCHARD)
JANES. James Roy died November 11, 1896. He left one child:

   a. EDNA LARRISON, born September 7, 1894. She married, October
     15, 1912, JOHN BRANT. She died December 16, 1925.

4. GRACE MAY LARRISON, born Sept. 20, 1879, died February 10, 1921.
Married November 25, 1903, WILLIAM H. PLANK, born November
14, 1878, son of SPENCER BEEBE and SARAH (McLEAN) PLANK.
They resided in Westfield, Pa. MR. WILLIAM H. PLANK married (2)
October 10, 1925, ETHEL B. KELLER and they reside in Benton, Pa.,
where he is engaged in the hardware business. One child was born
to the first marriage:

   a. MARIAN PLANK, born June 30, 1905. Married December 24, 1923,
     HERMAN M. HESS. They live in Wellsville, N. Y., where he is
     employed in Scoville and Brown's Wholesale Grocery Store and
     she is the organist in the Methodist Church. MR. HERMAN
     HESS is the son of ARCHER and ELIZABETH HESS of Wells-
     ville, N. Y.

Louise Brownell

IX. RACHEL LOUISE BROWNELL, ninth child of Verauns and Margaret Lewis (Jenkins) Brownell, was born in Angelica N. Y., August 23, 1848, and died in Chicago, Ill., October 14, 1883. Her childhood was spent mostly in Birdsall, N. Y. In 1868 she went to Genesee Wesleyan Seminary, Lima, N. Y., graduating in 1872. The following fall she went to Chicago to accept a position as teacher in the public schools in which work she continued until the time of her death. She was a devoted member of the Wabash Avenue Methodist Episcopal Church, where her unfaltering faith and unflagging zeal were an inspiration to all. She was an ardent worker in the Sunday School and its adjunct Mission School for the Chinese. Her loss was keenly felt by a large circle of co-workers, who most eloquently expressed their sorrow at her passing away at so youthful an age. Her body was brought back home and rests "in hope" in the cemetery in Scottsburg, N. Y. Her life was pure and beautiful and her death was radiant with glory ineffable.

Abigail Amanda Brow'nell McNinch

X. ABIGAIL AMANDA BROWNELL, born April 14, 1850, in
Birdsall, N. Y. Married January 1, 1874, in Groveland, N. Y.,
to EUGENE McNINCH of Scottsburg, N. Y. son of JOHN
McNINCH, born March 5, 1851. They have for many years
made their home in Westfield, Pa. They had one child:

1. ADA LOUISE McNINCH, born September 26, 1875, in Scottsburg, N. Y.
   She married (1) March 13, 1895, DELOS COOPER of Little Marsh,
   Pa., born August 23, 1875, and died May 11, 1911. MRS. COOPER
   married (2) —————, REV. EVAN BURTON of —————. He
   is son of —————. He is a Methodist minister and member of the Genesee Conference. Children by the first marriage were:

   a. LELAND EUGENE McNINCH, born September 13, 1896, and died
      September 26, 1901.

   b. LAWRENCE REID McNINCH, born April 13, 1904.

XI. A child, born December 18, 1852, and the mother and child
both died and were buried in the cemetery on the top of the
hill, Canaseraga, N. Y.

LOIS SHOWERS

VERANUS BROWNELL married as his second wife, LOIS B. SHOWERS of Urbana, N. Y., born December 20, 1828, and died February 14, 1906. The wedding day was August 11, 1853. Bravely she came to take charge of a home with a family of 10 children already in it, and the following additional children were born of this union, all at Birdsall, N. Y.

CATHERINE BROWNELL BENTLEY

1. CATHERINE LUCINDA BROWNELL, born June 25, 1855.
She attended the Nunda Academy when William H. Rogers was
principal there in 1874-5. Later she went to Chicago, Ill., and
with her half-sister, Louise, carried on quite an extensive mil-
linery business. August 11, 1887, she married FRANK TAG-
GERT BENTLEY of Chicago, Ill., born May 2, 1862, son of
FRANK W. and CATHERINE (TAYLOR) BENTLEY.
They lived in Chicago, Ill., for over 40 years. They are now
residing in Fort Meyers, Fla. Mr. Bentley was born and
raised on a farm and has engaged in the following occupations—
viz: School Teacher, Teamster, Gold Miner, Big Game Hunt-
er, Railway Clerk, Freight Agent, Terminal Superintendent,
Commercial Agent, Traffic Manager of Consolidated Steel Wire
Co., Illinois Steel Co., Universal Portland Cement Co. and at
present Consultant Traffic Manager of the Illinois Steel Co.
and the Universal Atlas Cement Co.

JASPER MORSE BROWNELL

II. JASPER MORSE BROWNELL, born in Birdsall, N. Y., May 25, 1862, married, November 17, 1888, GRACE COLTON of Hunts, N. Y., born August 16, 1872, the daughter of MARTIN SIMPSON and MARTHA LAVINA (MERITHEW) COLTON. He moved with his parents to Westfield, Pa., where they lived for two years. From there to Farmington and Short Tract and then to the old Homestead at Birdsall, where they lived until he was 17 years of age. His mother bought a place in Wayland. Here he attended High School and clerked in a grocery store. After a few years' experience on a farm, during which time he was married, he moved in the year 1907 back to Wayland, where he continued to live for several years. His children attended school and he engaged in business and held several local political offices, being Mayor of the Village for two years. In 1926 he took over the hardware store at Webster's Crossing for J. B. Conrad and here the family make their home. Their children were:

1. ALLIE M. BROWNELL, born November 17, 1889, died April 5, 1890.

2. MABEL COLTON BROWNELL, born June 14, 1892, in Birdsall, N. Y. Married August 21, 1914, HARRY L. JOHNSTON of Nunda, N. Y., born January 3, 1893, son of CONRAD and JANE ANN (WALLACE) JOHNSTON of Sparta, N. Y. HARRY L. JOHNSTON and family live in Wayland, N. Y. The first pair of boots that CONRAD JOHNSTON can remember of buying were made by VERANUS BROWNELL. Their children were:

a. ERNEST BROWNELL JOHNSTON, born August 7, 1915.

b. GRACE JUNE JOHNSTON, born July 2, 1917.

c. JASPER EVERETT JOHNSTON, born October 27, 1918, died in infancy.

d. FLORENCE HELEN JOHNSTON, born October 9, 1920.

e. KATHRYN RUTH JOHNSTON, born July 22, 1927.

3. HERBERT SIMPSON BROWNELL, born October 31, 1893, in Wayland, N. Y. Graduated from the Wayland High School June 20, 1913. Business career started June 23, 1913, as clerk in general offices of Illinois Steel Co., Chicago, Ill. Served in the 86th (Blackhawk) Division, Expeditionary Forces, World War. Honorable discharge as first sergeant, Company "C," 332 Machine Gun Batallion, February 1, 1919, Rockford, Ill. Salesman for Universal Portland Cement Co. until November 15 1921. Entered Mortgage Banking business

on that date as a bond salesman. At present assistant secretary and sales manager of that company. Member of the Loyal Lodge, 1007, F. & A. M., Oriental Consistory and Medina Temple, A. A. O. N. M. S., and the Hamilton Club of Chicago, Ill. He married October 19, 1921, RUTH RITCHIE, born May 1, 1897, daughter of CHARLES THOMAS and ORIE (HENRY) RITCHIE (married July 22, 1896). They live at 6901 Lakewood Ave., Chicago, Ill. HERBERT SIMPSON BROWN-ELL'S home address is No. 2642 Greenleaf Ave., Chicago, ,Ill. They have the following children:

a. PATRICIA RUTH BROWNELL, born December 17, 1922.

b. THOMAS RITCHIE BROWNELL, born April 3, 1926.

4. DORA IRENE BROWNELL, born 1894, died September 9, 1897.

5. JASPER EVERETT BROWNELL, born November 5, 1896. He graduated from the Wayland High School 1923. Took a business course at Genesee Wesleyan Seminary at Lima, N. Y. Graduated 1924. Is assistant cashier in the First National Bank of Atlanta, N. Y. He is unmarried.

6. HENRY COLTON BROWNELL, born September 30, 1898. Graduated from Lima Seminary 1924. Served three years in the World War. Was stationed at Newport Training Station from April 27 to July 14, 1918. Served on Transport "Pocohontas" and then on the "Shawmut," a mine laying boat, and was in the North Sea when the Armistice was signed. He was honorably discharged in July, 1920. Is working in Gunlocks Chair Factory in Wayland. Unmarried.

7. JOHN MARION BROWNELL, born September 4, 1900, in Birdsall, N. Y. Served in the World War. Was stationed at Newport, R. I., and then was on Transport "Antigua." Was honorably discharged in December, 1918. He is coach of athletics and physical director of Haverling High School, Bath, N. Y. He is not married.

8. THEODORE WILSON BROWNELL, born 1908, died January 25, 1909.

9. CLAIR VERANUS BROWNELL, born July 3, 1910, in Wayland, N. Y. Married February 16, 1928, MARCENA RINGER daughter of CHARLES and EVA (————) RINGER of Hornell. They have one child:

a. JOAN LOUISE BROWNELL, born July 16, 1929.

FRANK ELMER BROWNELL

III. FRANK ELMER BROWNELL, born February 29, 1864, and
died November 28, 1912. He was born at the Old Homestead
at Birdsall, where his youth was spent working on the farm.
He married in 1897 LUCY GERTRUDE FARNHAM, born
April 6, 1879, and died in California November 17, 1920. She
was the daughter of JAMES FARNHAM and AMELIA
ROGERS (sister of Wm. H. Rogers). Frank and Gertrude
made their home in Canaseraga, N. Y., where he engaged in
the coal, Wood and Produce business. They were members
of the M. E. Church in Canaseraga. Their children were born
there as follows:

1 OLIVE BROWNELL, born 1898, died in 1899.

2. RITA BROWNELL, born 1899, died in 1900.

3. ONNOLEE ALETA BROWNELL, born September 13, 1903. Married August
25, 1924, RALPH GRAHAM KRETSCHMAR, born March 23, 1893, son of
HERMAN RUDOLPH and ISABELLE (GRAHAM) KRETSCHMAR. Address
No. 775 Park Ave., New York City.

4. FRANK BENTLEY BROWNELL, born February 9, 1911. Lives in California. (No record.)

5. FRANK ELMER BROWNELL, born March, 1913, died in August, 1913.

JOSEPH VERANUS BROWNELL

IV. JOSEPH FLINT BROWNELL, born May 1, 1867, on the old
Homestead Farm at Birdsall, N. Y. He married, June 14, 1887,
in Canaseraga, N. Y., Anna Robinson, born April 14, 1871,
daughter of Fayette Robinson and Miranda Robinson. They
made their home in Canaseraga, N. Y., where Joseph was at
first in business with his brother, Frank. After the death of
Frank, Joseph carried on the business alone. Their children
were:

1. ETHEL MAY BROWNELL, born April 10, 1890, died 1917. Married
   July 4, 1907, MERTON SPENCER, son of JAMES SPENCER and LYDIA
   SPENCER. Children:

   a. HARLAN SPENCER, born May, 1908.

   b. MARION SPENCER, born August, 1910.

   c. HUGH SPENCER, born September, 1912.

   d. JOSEPH SPENCER, born September, 1913.

   e. LESTER SPENCER, born September, 1915.

2. LYNN ROBINSON BROWNELL, born December 17, 1897.

3. LESTER JOHN BROWNELL, born August 24, 1898. Married June 8,
   1927, MARGARET GROSSE.

4. GRACE IRENE BROWNELL, born June 23, 1905. Married December 21,
   1923, JAMES RUSSELL BAILEY, son of JAMES BAILEY and ENNA
   BAILEY. Children:

   a. JAMES RUSSELL BAILEY, JR., born September 18, 1924.

   b. WALTER BAILEY, born September 7, 1926.

5. MYRTLE JOSEPHINE BROWNELL, born March 14, 1909.

ALLEN

I. SAMUEL ALLEN, of Braintree, Mass., lived there in 1632. He was made a Freeman in 1635. After a few years he removed to Bridgewater, Mass. His wife's given name was Ann. Her maiden name is not given. He died in September, 1669. She died in September, 1641. Their children were:

1. SAMUEL ALLEN, born 1633. See below.

2. MARY ALLEN, born ————. Married 1656, NATHANIEL GREEN-WOOD.

3. SARAH ALLEN, born March 30, 1639. Married JOSIAH STANDISH of Duxbury.

4. Child born August, 1641. Died September, 1641. ANN died Septembe, 1641, and SAMUEL ALLEN married for a second wife, MARGARET ————, widow of EDWARD LAMB, and they had children:

5. JAMES ALLEN, born ————.

6. ABIGAIL ALLEN, born ————. Married, 1670, JOHN CARY.

7. JOSEPH ALLEN, born May 15, 1650.

II. SAMUEL ALLEN, No. 1 above, married, 1658, Sarah, daughter of George Partridge of Duxbury. He was a careful and painstaking town clerk for many years. The records of Bridgewater, Mass., bear witness to his excellent work. He was Representative in 1693. Their children were:

1. SAMUEL ALLEN, born 1660. Married, 1685, to REBECCA CARY, daughter of JOHN CARY. REBECCA CARY—See below.

2. ASAHEL (Essiel) ALLEN, born, 1663.

3. MEHITABLE ALLEN, born 1665. Married ISAAC ALDEN

4. SARAH ALLEN, born, 1667. Married, first, JONATHAN CARY, died 1695; second, BENJAMIN SNOW, 1705.

5. BETHIA ALLEN, born 1669. Married JOHN PRYOR.

6. NATHANIEL ALLEN, born 1672. Married, 1696, BETHEL CONANT.

7. EBENEZER ALLEN, born 1674. Married REBECCA SKATE.

8. JOSIAH ALLEN, born 1677. Married, 1707, MARY READ.

9. ELISHA ALLEN, born 1679. Married, 1701, MEHITABLE BYRAM.

10. NEHEMIAH ALLEN, born 1681. Married, 1707, SARAH WAMIEL.

III. SAMUEL ALLEN, No. 1 above, born 1660. Married, 1685, REBECCA CARY of Bridgewater, Mass., daughter of John Cary and Elizabeth Godfrey. Their children were:

1. SAMUEL ALLEN, born 1686. Married, 1728, JANE TURNER, died, 1750.

2. EPHRIAM ALLEN, born 1689.

3. TIMOTHY ALLEN, born 1691. See below.

4. JOSEPH ALLEN, born 1693, died without issue.

5. MEHITABLE ALLEN, born 1694. Married ———— BUSHNELL.

6. ————, child born 1697, died in infancy and the mother died also.

IV. TIMOTHY ALLEN, No. 2 above. Lived in Norwich, Conn., and later in Windham, Conn. He married, in 1714, Rachel Bushnell, daughter of Joseph Bushnell and Mary Leffingwell of Norwich, Conn. Their oldest son was:

1. DANIEL ALLEN, born 1717, in Norwich, Conn.

V. DANIEL ALLEN, eldest son of Timothy Allen and Rachel Bushnell, was born in Norwich, Conn., in 1717. In young manhood he moved to Ashford, Conn. Here he met with a young lady of his own age, Azubah Ladd, born in Haverhill, N. H., daughter of David and Hepzibah (Hazen) Ladd, a famous family of Haverhill. Daniel and Azubah were married October 13, 1741. Their second daughter was:

1. RACHEL ALLEN, born July 21, 1746, in Ashford, Conn.

VI. RACHEL ALLEN, born as above stated. She married JOHN
CHEEDLE as his second wife, early in 1769, as they were received into the Church in Ashford together in that year, and
their first child was born in 1670. They were married by Rev.
Timothy Allen, uncle of Rachel Allen and pastor of the Church
in Ashford. For the continuation of this record see "Cheedle"
Family.

BUSHNELL

I. FRANCIS BUSHNELL, SR., and Francis Bushnell, Jr., father and son, were among the first settlers of Guilford. Francis, Sr., signed the plantation contract. He was born in England in 1576 and died in Guilford in 1646. He married in England in 1597, Rebecca Holmes. They lived on a home lot of three acres and had for neighbors, John Hoadley, William Dudley and Thomas Jordan. Among his descendants are David Bushnell, who invented the first torpedo, The American Turtle, and Cornelius Bushnell, who advanced the money with which Ericsson built the "Monitor." The children of Francis Bushnell and Rebecca Holmes were: (not in the order of their birth)

1. FRANCIS BUSHNELL, born 1609, died December 9, 1681. Married MARY WHITE.

2. REBECCA BUSHNELL, born ————, died ————. Married JOHN LORD in Guilford, 1646.

3. WILLIAM BUSHNELL, born ————, died 1683. Married REBECCA CHAPMAN. (Jessie's line see below.)

4. RICHARD BUSHNELL, born ————, died 1657. Married MARY MARVIN, 1645. (My line see below.)

5. JOHN BUSHNELL, born ————, died 1667.

6. SARAH BUSHNELL, born ————, baptized November 26, 1625, in Howfield, Essex, England. Married July 14, 1642, REV. JOHN HOADLEY of Guilford. They both returned to England and died there. Two of their grandsons, JOHN and BENJAMIN HOADLEY, were Bishops of the Church of England.

II. RICHARD BUSHNELL (No. 4 above) of Saybrook, married, in 1629, MARY MARVIN, daughter of Matthew Marvin. Their children were:

1. JOSEPH BUSHNELL, born 1651, died 1748. Married MARY LEFFING-
WELL. (See "Leffingwell" Family.)

2. RICHARD BUSHNELL, born 1652, died 1727. Married ELIZABETH AD-
GATE.

3. FRANCIS BUSHNELL, born 1654, died ————. Twin.

4. MARY BUSHNELL, born 1654, died ————. Twin. Married THOMAS
LEFFINGWELL, JR.

5. MARCIE BUSHNELL, born 1657, died ————. (Also called MARIA.)
Married, first, 1678, JONATHAN BUDD; second, DEACON JOSEPH CARY.

III. JOSEPH BUSHNELL (No. 1 above), born 1651, died 1748.
Married Mary Leffingwell. Children as follows:

1. MARY BUSHNELL, born 1675, died ————.

2. JOSEPH BUSHNELL, born 1677, died ————.

3. JONATHAN BUSHNELL, born 1679. Married, first, MARY CALKINSON;
second, MARY BLISS; third, HANNAH ————.

4. DANIEL BUSHNELL, born 1681, died 1681.

5. DEBORAH BUSHNELL, born 1682, died ————. Married JOHN LANE

6. HANNAH BUSHNELL, born 1684, died ————.

7. NATHAN BUSHNELL, born 1686, died ————. Married, first, ANNE
CAREY; second, MEHITABLE ALLEN. Six children.

8. REBECCA BUSHNELL, born 1688, died ————. Married JOB BAR-
STOW.

9. ABIGAIL BUSHNELL, born 1690, died ————. Married JOSEPH CARY
(DEACON JOSEPH) of Windham, Conn.

10. RACHEL BUSHNELL, born 1692. Married in 1714, TIMOTHY ALLEN
(see page ——) of Norwich, Conn. He died 1755.

11. JERUSHA BUSHNELL, born 1695, died ————. Married JOHN
HOTCHKISS.

IV. RACHEL BUSHNELL. Married Timothy Allen and became
the mother of Daniel Allen, who was the second Great-Grand-
father of my mother. (See chart page.)

CAREY

In Domesday Book, under date of 1198, Kerri of Torr Abbey is a Tenant in chief. The name also appears in ancient records as "Kari" or "Karry." An Adam de Kari, or Karry, 1170, was Lord of the Castle Karry in Somerset, and the Carys of Devonshire are regarded as of the same family. In 1270 the name appears as de Karry, but by the next century the "de" has disappeared, and Carey, or Cary, becomes the correct orthography. For the last few centuries Cary has been the most common form of spelling. "Carew" is considered by some authorities as one and the same name as Carey, and the story is told of two Walter Carews, members at the same time of the House of Commons, that it was proposed that one should be called CAREY and the other CAREW, in order to prevent embarrassing situations and to end the confusion.

> "What Care I?
> and
> What Care You?"

was their reply. The history of one branch of the Cary family in America begins with Col. Wilson Myler Cary, son of John and grandson of William Cary, Lord Mayor of Bristol in 1611. Myler received a grant of 3000 acres of land in Westmoreland, Va., in 1654. "Colonel" was the title he brought with him and he earned the title of "Major" here. His tombstone at Cary's quarters in Warwick bears the Coat of Arms herewith presented. His wife was Alice, daughter of Henry Hobson, Alderman of Bristol, and they had four sons and three daughters. Miles, the immigrant, came over as early as 1640. He was a member of the King's Council, under Berkeley. This line claims as ancestor Sir William Cary, who fell at Tewkesbury in 1471. His son, Sir Thomas Cary, married a granddaughter of the Duke of Somerset. Their son, Sir William Cary, married Mary, sister of Anne Boleyn, Queen. Henry Cary, their son, was Lord Hemsdon, the Honest Courtier, of Elizabeth's reign. The Carys formerly held two earldoms, Monmouth and Dover, also the barony of Humdon and Henry Cary, born 1622, was the first viscount of Falkland. In New England, JOHN CARY'S name is found in Plymouth records in 1634, the year of his arrival. Helped found Duxbury and Bridgewater. In 1656 he was Constable of the latter place. the first and only officer of the town that year. From 1657 until his death in 1681, he was Town Clerk. According to tradition, he was the first Teacher of Latin in the Plymouth Colony. His sons and grandsons were, like himself, founders of towns in New England. They were also Pioneers in Pennsylvania. "The Society of the Descendants of John Cary" keeps green the family name by Annual Reunions, and have erected a handsome marker at West Bridgewater on the site of John, the Pilgrim's home. John Cary's wife was Elizabeth Godfrey and their children numbered twelve. John Cary was credited with various sums for garrison duty at Dunstable, Mass. Soldier of King Philip's War (see Bodge page 359) Plymouth County records Vol. XI p. 245 under date of July 10, 1677, he is called Sergeant Cary of Bridgewater, Mass. He appears always to have been active in public affairs. The following is a list of his children:

1. JOHN CARY, born 1645, died ———. Married.

2. FRANCIS CARY, born 1647, died ———. Married.

3. MARY CARY, born 1653, died ———. Married.

4. JONATHAN CARY, born 1656, died ———. Married.

5. DAVID CARY, born 1658, died ———. Married.

6. HANNAH CARY, born 1661, died ———. Married.

7. JOSEPH CARY, born 1663, died ———. Married.

8. REBECCA CARY, born 1665, died ———. Married, 1685, SAMUEL ALLEN.

9. SARAH CARY, born 1667, died ———. Married.

10. MEHITABLE CARY, born 1670, died———. Married, MILES STANDISH, a descendent of Mayflower STANDISH line.

For a record of the children of REBECCA ALLEN, No. 8 above, and the pedigree of SAMUEL ALLEN, see "ALLEN" Family.

CHEEDLE

I. GEORGE CHEEDLE, with his brother, Asa, came to America from England in 1720 and settled in Lebanon, Conn. Another passenger on the same boat was Miss Martha Burge and on the way over a friendship was begun, which ripened into love and within a few months George and Martha were married. The wedding day was August 16, 1721, and record of the marriage may be found in the vital statistics of Lebanon, Vol. 1, page 47, and their nine children are recorded in Vol. A, page 9. George Cheedle was a member of Adonijah Fitch's company of Connecticut Militia from New London, which went to the capture of Louisburg Fortress, Cape Breton Island, July 6, 1745. He was dismissed from service October 9, but died before reaching home. Of course, he was dismissed on account of illness. There is a statement in the American Magazine for February, 1905, page 141, that he fought at Quebec, and was honorably discharged but died before reaching home. Of course, both statements cannot be true. My own opinion, formed from a few clews in the records, is that he fought at both places and that he died in the year 1759, after, or during the battle of Quebec. (See Council of Appointments, Vol. IV, pages ———.) In the list of nine children above referred to, No. 5 was:

II. JOHN CHEEDLE, who was born in Lebanon, Conn., August 16, 1732, and died in Pomfret, Vt., October 20, 1805. While still a young man, John went from Lebanon and setttled in Pomfret,Conn. Here he married Mary Bosworth in 1761, and their children were:

1. JOHN CHEEDLE, born ———, died ———. Married ———.

2. TIMOTHY CHEEDLE, born ———, died ———. Married ———.

3. BOSWORTH CHEELE, born ———, died ———. Married ———.

4. MARY CHEEDLE, born ———, died ———. Married ———.

The record of the baptism of these four children may be found in the Congregational Church records of Ashford, Conn. I have not found the record of Mary Bosworth's death. But the church records just referred to show that John Cheedle and his second wife, Rachel Allen, were received into the Church in 1769, as were also his brother, Asa, and his wife, Martha Paddock. Both the above couples were married by the Rev. Timothy Allen, uncle of Rachel Allen, and pastor of the Church at Ashford. We also find in the same records the account of the dismissal of John and Asa Cheedle and their wives to Pomfret, Vermont. Now, in-as-much as the scene is to shift to the hilly country of northern Vermont, we will give a little history of the settlement of the place where they settled. They called the place Pomfret after the name of the place they had left in Connecticut. Most of the original settlers came from that place. A few of them, however, came from Woodstock and Sutton, Mass. The organization was effected on the first Monday in September, 1761, with Zachariah Waldo as chairman. The first survey and division of lots was made by Simeon Sessions and Isaac Dana (Sarah, daughter of Simeon Sessions, was the wife of Isaac Dana) in 1770. The same committee rearranged the lots in 1771. The boundary line between Pomfret and Woodstock was finally settled in 1778. It was a constant wonder to us (My wife and I), when we visited Pomfret in the Summer of 1924, how our ancestors ever succeeded in making their way up the Connecticut River and then up and over the Mountains (for such they really are), to so inaccessible a location. The scenery *is*, indeed, beautiful, but so precipitous and rocky are the mountains that we were not surprised to find the lots which fell to Joseph Brownell (father of Veranus Brownell) utterly abandoned now. Here, however, they did settle, and here John Cheedle and Rachel Allen raised the following family of children:

1. RACHEL CHEEDLE, born 1770, died 1777. The first death in Pomfret, Vt.

2. ASA CHEEDLE, born 1772, died ————. Married POLLY ALDRICH.

3. DANIEL CHEEDLE, born 1774, died 1777.

4. MARTHA CHEEDLE, born 1776, died ————.

5. RACHEL CHEEDLE, born 1778, died ————. Married JOSEPH BROWN-
   ELL.

6. DANIEL CHEEDLE, born 1780. Twin.

7. GEORGE CHEEDLE, born 1780. Twin.

8. AZUBA CHEEDLE, born 1782, died ————. Married ZEBEDEE CHURCH-
   ILL.

9. HEPZIBAH CHEEDLE, born 1784, died ————. Married EZEKIEL
   BURNHAM.

10. ELIZABETH CHEEDLE, born 1787.

John Cheedle was a soldier in the Revolutionary War. The record of his service may be seen in the Vermont Rolls of Revolutionary Soldiers. His brother, Asa, also served in the Revolution.

III. RACHEL CHEEDLE, No. 5 above. Married Joseph Brownell, June 11, 1809. On March 16, 1810, their first and only baby was born. His name was VERANUS. Ten days later the mother died. For further record see "Brownell" Family and Chart No. III.

CORLISS

0━━━━━━━━0

1. GEORGE CORLISS, the founder of the family in this country, was born in Devonshire, England, in 1617. He was son of Thomas Corliss. Before he attained his majority, he, like many others of his time, turned longing eyes toward the opportunities of the great new Western World. Like his famous descendant, seven generations down, viz, George Henry Corliss, the inventor of the steam engine, he knew how to bring things to pass and make dreams come true. So in 1639 he embarked on his great adventure, and came to New England, where he settled first in Newbury, Mass., but soon removed to Haverhill, settling there in 1640 in West Parish, on the place later known as "Poplar Lawn Farm." Here the remainder of his life was passed. He was one of the first settlers and his name appears on the list of freemen in 1645. He was Selectman in years 1648 to 1652, and again in 1657-1659 and 1669. He was Constable in 1650. His will was dated October 18, 1686, and he died the following day. His beautiful home remained in the possession of the family for several generations. By a strange co-incidence he and his son, John, and his grandson, John, all died while sitting in the same chair. George Corliss married October 26, 1645, at Haverhill, Joanna Davis, daughter of Thomas Davis. And their children were:

1. MARY* CORLISS, born 1646, died ————. Married 1663, WILLIAM NEFF.

2. JOHN CORLISS, born ————, died ————. Married ————.

3. DEBORAH CORLISS, born ————, died ————. Married ————.

4. MARTHA CORLISS, born 1649, died 1698. Married 1674, SAMUEL LADD.

For the continuation of this record see "LADD" family.

*Mary Neff, with Mrs. Hannah Dustin, gained her freedom from the Indians when they had been taken captive, by despatching ten out of twelve of their captors with the tomahawk. For which brave deed a monument has been erected to their memory in Haverhill. They and their families were also rewarded by gifts of land, and also of silver tankards and goblets from Governor Nicholson of Maryland. We share in the honor of being descended from a family, one of whom proved her courage and bravery by taking part in so dangerous and terrible a deed for her life and liberty. Mrs. Dustin was a sister-in-law of Mary Neff. Their husbands were away fighting the Indians. Mrs. Dustin had a little baby three weeks old. Mrs. Neff had been taking care of her. When the Indians captured them they dashed the baby's brains out against the tree and compelled the women to walk a great distance without stopping for rest. Then when the Indians were all asleep around a camp fire the two women quietly arose and, seizing tomahawks, inflicted swift and sure death upon five each, one on each side awakened by the confusion escaped. The monument above referred to bears the image of a woman wielding a tomahawk, while the record is inscribed on the base.

CORNELL

At first the name was written "Cornwall." Then for a time it was written Cornewell. The first Earldom was conferred by

I. KING JOHN (he who signed "Magna Charta," no thanks to him, however, for he tried hard enough to overthrow it, even after he had affixed the royal seal) upon his son,

II. RICHARD, in 1216, and he became the first Earl of Cornwall and thus the name was started.

III. SIR JOHN CORNWALL, son of Richard and grandson of King John married Elizabeth, daughter of John of Gaunt, Duke of Lancaster, and his wife, the sister of King Edward IV. Sir John died in 1243 and the title now passes down through three (IV and V) succeeding Earls of Corwall to

VI. JOHN CORNWALL, Gent., who married Jane Varney. He died April 12, 1561 and his son, who is No.

VII. THOMAS CORNEWALL, owner of the Manor of Fairsted in Essex, succeeded to the Earldom. His son,

VIII. HUMPHREY CORNEWALL, was the next Earl and his son,

IX. JOHN CORNEWALL, was the next and was the father of

X. THOMAS CORNELL, the American Ancestor, born 1695, in Essex, England, married Rebecca Briggs (sister of John of whom more later); died 1655. Rebecca was born 1600 and died February 8, 1673. He came to America in 1638 with his wife and children, settled in Boston, where by a vote of the town meeting he is permitted "to buy of William Boulston, his house, yard and garden at the back side of Mr. Coddington's lot, and to become an inhabitant." This property was situated on Washington St., between Sumner St. and Milk St. He sold it in 1643 to Edward Tyng. On September 6, 1638, Thomas Cornell was licensed to keep an inn in the room of William Boulston till the next General Court. Thomas was associated with Roger Williams and Mr. Throckmorton in the settlement of the Antinomian Controversy in New Amsterdam. Roger Williams went to England and secured a charter for this colony. They secured grants of land and permits for peaceful possession from Governor Winthrop and the Dutch Government. Some trouble ensued with the Indians owing to the unwise actions of Governor Keifts in which the "Indians destroyed many buildings by fire and killed many whites." Roger Williams said, "Mine eyes saw the flames in these towns, and the flights of the hurrying men, women and children." Governor Winthrop said, "By the intervention of Roger Williams the Indians were pacified and peace re-established." Thomas Cornell suffered the loss of his buildings and stock and Mr. and Mrs. (Ann) Hutchinson were killed. As a result of this loss Thomas returned to Rhode Island, and February 4, 1646, secured a grant of 100 acres of land from the Town of Portsmouth on the south side of the River Wading, to run from the river to the land of Edward Hutchinson (son of Ann). This may be considered the original home of the Cornells and it has never passed out of the hands of the family. In the "Friends" records of February, 1773, we read, "Rebecca Cornell, widow of Thomas Cornell, was strangely killed in her own house at Portsmouth. The body was twice "viewed" by the coroner, buried, digged up and re-interred by the side of her husband." On May 23rd following her son, Thomas 2, was charged with the murder and after a trial which reads like the farce that it was, was convicted and hung. Among the witnesses, was John Briggs, the brother of Rebecca. He swore that she appeared to him after her death and said, "See how I was burned with fire." It appears that she was sitting by the fire, smoking a pipe, and that she probably fell asleep, and the pipe fell into her lap and set her clothing on fire. It was inferred that someone set her on fire, and as her son, Thomas, was the last one with her, and as she had a little property which would have gone to the son, but, if he were out of the way, would go to the brother, John, he was interested in fixing the blame on the son—hence his peculiar testimony. In fact, he did get the property. Durfee, in his "Legal Tracts of Rhode Island," says that this was most unjust execution in the annals of R. I. The children of Thomas and Rebecca were:

1 THOMAS CORNELL, born about 1618, in England, and married, first, a wife whose name we cannot find. He married, second, SARAH EARLE.

2. SARAH CORNELL, born about 1620. Was married three times, first, 1643, THOMAS WILLETT; second, 1647, CHARLES BRIDGES; third, 1682, JOHN LAWRENCE.

3. REBECCA CORNELL, born 1622, died 1713. Married, 1647, GEORGE WOOLSEY.

4. ANN CORNELL, born ————, died ————. Married THOMAS KENT.

5. RICHARD CORNELL, born ————, died 1694. Married ELIZA-BETH ————.

6. JOHN CORNELL, born ————, died 1704. Married MARY RUSSELL.

7. JOSHUA CORNELL, born ————. No record.

8. ELIZABETH CORNELL, born ————. Married CHRISTOPHER ALMY.

9. SAMUEL CORNELL, born ————, died 1715.

II. THOMAS CORNELL, no. 1 above, born about 1618; died May 23, 1673. Married twice, first unknown; second, Sarah Earle. In 1655 we find his name in the Portsmouth, R. I. records as Thomas Cornell, Jr. A number of records bearing his name are found. He was Deputy of the General Court in 1664 to 1672. He was Auditor for the Colony. He was Special Messenger to the Governor of Plymouth from the General Court of Rhode Island. He was appointed by the General Court to treat with the Indians in regard to purchasing land for the Extension of the Boundaries of Rhode Island. His will names his wife, "Sarah" and provides that she and her children shall have one-half of his estate, and his children by his first wife shall have the other half. The children were:

By the first wife:

1. THOMAS CORNELL, born 1653, died 1714. Married SUSANNA LAWTON.

2. EDWARD CORNELL, born ————, died 1708. Married MARY ————.

3. STEPHEN CORNELL, born 1656, died 1673. Married HANNAH MOSHIER.

4. JOHN CORNELL, born ————, died ————. Married HANNAH SMITH..

And by the second wife, SARAH EARLES:

5. ————, a daughter. No record.

6. ————, a daughter. No record.

7. INNOCENT CORNELL, born October 24, 1673, and died July, 1732, two months after her father's death. Probably her name was a protest against her father's unjust execution.

III. THOMAS CORNELL, No. 1 above, born 1653; died 1714. Married Susanna Lawton. His name is found in the records of Portsmouth many times, on deeds, wills and other legal papers. In 1683 he was Deputy from Portsmouth and was Justice in 1705. He was Assistant Governor of R. I. in 1726 (the same as senator now). His children were:

1. THOMAS CORNELL, born 1674, died 1728. Married MARTHA FREEBORN.

2. GEORGE CORNELL, born 1676, died 1752. He married three times, viz: first, PHILADELPHIA EASTIS; second, DELIVERANCE CLARK; third, ABIGAIL SISSON.

3. ELIZABETH CORNELL, born 1690, died 1750. Married SAMUEL CRANSTON.

IV. GEORGE CORNELL, No. 2 above. For record see No. 2. Name occurs on deeds and other legal papers in Portsmouth. He was admitted freeman in 1696. He was Assistant to the Governor 1709 to 1716. Deputy to the General Court 1709 to 1731. His children were:

By first wife:

1. RUTH CORNELL, born December 12, 1697. Married JOSEPH BROWNELL.

By second wife:

2. WALTER CORNELL, born 1700, died 1777. Married MARY NICHOLS.

3. PHILADELPHIA CORNELL, born 1702, died 1781. Married THOMAS COOK.

4. GEORGE CORNELL, born 1705, died ————. Married REBECCA HICKS.

5. THOMAS CORNELL, born 1707, died ————. Married DINAH ————.

6. RICHARD CORNELL, born 1709, died ————. Married MARY MARTIN.

7. JOB CORNELL, born 1710, died ————.

8. SUSANNA CORNELL, born 1712, died ————. Married WILLIAM BRIGHTMAN.

9. SARAH CORNELL, born 1713, died ————.

10. CLARK CORNELL, born 1714, died ————. Married PRISCILLA LAWTON.

11. JOSEPH CORNELL, born 1716, died 1732.

12. BENJAMIN CORNELL, born 1720, died 1732.

By third wife:

13. BENJAMIN CORNELL, born 1733, died ————. Married ELIZABETH BENNETT.

14. DELIVERANCE CORNELL, born 1738, died 1740.

15. SARAH CORNELL, born 1743, died ————. Married JOHN MANCHESTER.

16. JOB CORNELL, born 1747.

For continuation of this record, see "Brownell" Family.

EASTIS

The name is also spelled without the "a", viz—Estis or Estes. *Estes* *Wilson*

I. ROBERT EASTIS was of Newinton, East Kent, England. His wife's given name was DOROTHY. We have not found her maiden name or the list of their children. We know of only one son, that is the one who came to this country, viz:

II. MATTHEW EASTIS, born in Dover, England, in 1645, and died in this country in 1723. He married, about 1678, PHILADELPHIA JENCKS. They lived in Scituate, Mass. Matthew lived in Lynn, Mass., as early as 1695. But he was in New England in 1676 and probably before. He was a Mariner and a Quaker. Their children were:

  1. PHILADELPHIA EASTIS, born 1679, died 1698. Married, 1696, GEORGE CORNELL.

  2. JOSEPH EASTIS, born 1682, died ————. Married ————.

  3. JOHN EASTIS, born 1684, died ————. Married ————.

  4. RICHARD EASTIS, born 1686, died ————. Married ————.

  5. MATTHEW EASTIS, born 1689, died ————. Married ————.

III. PHILADELPHIA EASTIS, No. 1 above, born 1679; died 1698. Married, 1696, GEORGE CORNELL. She was his first wife. Her only child was Ruth (Cornell), born 1697, and the mother died soon thereafter. George Cornell married twice, the other two wives bearing him 15 children. For the list and the Cornell pedigree see "Cornell" Family.

FISH

In the settlement of the English Colonies in America, there were at least eight individuals who bore the name of Fish. They came from England and settled in various locations in the early part of the 17th century, and have become the progenitors of numerous families of that name scattered throughout the States. These eight were: Jonathan, John and Nathaniel, the first comers in the year 1637. They settled in Sandwich on Cape Cod and received grants of land there in 1640. THOMAS FISH settled in Portsmouth, R. I., in 1643 and died there in 1687. He was son of ROBERT FISH and ALICE FISH (own cousins) of Market Harborough in the Paris of Great Bowden, in Leicestershire, Eng. John Fish was living in Connecticut in 1651. William Fish in 1651 was living in Windser and died in Stonington in 1689. Joseph Fish of Stamford, Conn., 1651, a soldier in the Great Swamp Fight at Kingston, Conn., 1676. Edward Fish of Talbot Co. Md. prior to 1669; died 1696.

The first three mentioned were brothers, sons of Augustine Fish, and all the others were cousins. All were grandchildren of John Fish and his wife, Margaret Cradock. In the Parish Church, in the village of Great Bowden, a beautiful and picturesque building of stone, long and low, with heavy overhanging eaves, and sides and tower all covered with ivy, on the North wall of the chancel is a tablet erected to the memory of Henrietta Fish, wife of Augustine Fish, Gentleman, and daughter of Sir Edward Farmer, Knight, of Middlesex, who died in 1703. On this tablet are impaled the Arms of husband and wife, as follows: FISH, a chevron between 3 owls, engrailed and FARMER—Arms, sable, on a chevron between 3 lamps, arg. burning with flames, proper, 3 mullets, sable. This Augustine was a cousin of Thomas, the American immigrant. The line as disclosed by the records in this Church is as follows:

I. EDWARD FISH, who died in 1518 and whose wife's name was
　Agnes.

II. RICHARD FISH, son of above and father of

III. AUGUSTINE FISH, who died 1580, who was the father of

IV. JOHN FISH, whose wife was Margaret Cradock.　He died in
　1630.　Their children were:

　1. AUGUSTINE FISH, born, June 11, 1578.

　2. WILLIAM FISH, born March 9, 1580.

　3. KATHERINE FISH, born April 15, 1582.

　4. THOMAS FISH, born May 8, 1584, Wedgenock Park, Warwickshire.

　5. SARAH FISH, born Apr. 11, 1586.　Married JOHN JOHNSON.

　6. AMBROSE FISH, born July 6, 1588.

　7. MARY FISH, born December 20, 1589; died, 1591.

　8. ELIZABETH FISH, born November 15, 1591.

　9. FRANCIS FISH, born October 29, 1593.

　10. ANNE FISH, born June 2, 1596.

　11. ALICE FISH, born November 6, 1597.　She married ROBERT FISH, her
　　own cousin.　See below.

　12. MARY FISH, born December 8, 1599.

　13. JOHN FISH, born January 26, 1602; died, 1623.

　　The above ROBERT FISH, who married ALICE (No. 11), was the son
　　of THOMAS, who was the son of RICHARD, No. II in this Ancestral
　　Line.

V. ROBERT FISH, born 1593, and died 1639.　Married Alice, No.
　11 above.　Their children were:

　1. THOMAS FISH, born January 1, 1619.　The Immigrant lived in Ports-
　　mouth, R. I.

　2. JOHN FISH, born January 21, 1621.

3. RUTH FISH, born September 1, 1622.

4. MARY FISH, born January 24, 1624; died 1624.

5. MARY FISH, born April 25, 1625.

6. JOSEPH FISH, born September 17, 1626.

7. NATHAN FISH, born March 7, 1629; died 1631.

8. TABITHA FISH, born May 8, 1630; died 1631.

9. HANNAH FISH, born November 24, 1633.

10. CHRISTIAN FISH, born December 10, 1637.

11. BENJAMIN FISH, born August 11, 1639.

VI. THOMAS FISH, No. 1 above, born January 1, 1619; died 1699. Married MARY SHERMAN. Lived in Portsmouth, R. I. He was a blacksmith. The records of him which we find are just the ordinary experiences of life, as follows: 1643 he was given a grant of land by the Portsmouth officials; 1655 he was made a freeman. In the years 1660 and 1662 signed deeds and collected rents. In 1665, on the 20th day of February, he sold land. In 1674, he was made a member of the Town Council. In 1684-85 and 1692 deeded land to son and grandson. In 1687-1692 and 1699 made wills, revoking all except the last one, which was proved the same year and which mentions wife and living children. Their children were:

1. THOMAS FISH, born ————, died 1684. Married GRIZZEL STRANGE.

2. MEHITABLE FISH, born ————, died ————. Married, 1667, JOSEPH TRIPP.

3. MARY FISH, born ————, died 1747. Married, 1671, FRANCES BRAYTON.

4. ALICE FISH, born ————, died 1734. Married WILLIAM KNOWLES.

5. JOHN FISH, born ————, died 1742. Married JOANNA ————.

6. DANIEL FISH, born ————, died 1723. Married ABIGAIL MUMFORD.

7. ROBERT FISH, born ————, died 1730. Married MARY HALL.

VI. ROBERT FISH, No. 7 above, born ————; died 1730. Married, 1686, MARY HALL, daughter of Zuriel and Elizabeth (Tripp) Hall. He followed the same occupation as his father, viz. blacksmith, and lived in Portsmouth, R. I. He was made a freeman in 1686. He served on Juries in the years 1694, '99 and 1707. He was elected Pound Keeper in the years 1705, '6, 7, '8, '9. In 1735, he was made a Lieut. and died that year. His children were:

1. ROBERT FISH, born 1690, died ————. Married ANNE PALMER.

2. MARY FISH, born 1693, died ————. Married, 1710, THOMAS DEXTER.

3. WILLIAM FISH, born 1695, died 1764. Married, 1716, MARY BENNETT.

4. ZURIEL FISH, born 1697, died 1728.

5. ISAAC FISH, born 1699, died 1728.

6. ALICE FISH, born 1702, died 1756. Married, 1725, NATHANIEL PECK.

7. JONATHAN FISH, born 1704, died ————. Married 1726, MICHAL RHODES.

8. DANIEL FISH, born 1707, died ————. Married, 1730, MARY TALLMAN.

9. DAVID FISH, born 1710, died 1781. Married JEMIMA TALLMAN.

VII. DAVID FISH, No. 9 above. He lived in Portsmouth, R. I., and was a blacksmith as his father and grandfather had been before him. He married, 1730, Jemima Tallman, daughter of James and Hannah (Swain) Tallman. He died suddenly in his chair just after remarking that he "could not do more for his family if he lived." In December, 1778, his daughter, Patience, wrote in a diary that her father then had 17 grandchildren buried and 73 living and 8 great-grandchildren living and that he was then 68 years old. His children were:

1. MARY FISH, born 1732, died 1793. Married, 1749, ISAAC LAWTON.

2. HANNAH FISH, born 1733, died ————. Married, 1757, BORDEN CHASE.

3. DAVID FISH, born 1734, died 1779. Married, 1757, LYDIA DENNIS.

4. CHRISTOPHER FISH, born 1736, died 1779. Married ————.

5. CHARITY FISH born 1738, died 1821. Married, 1760, GEORGE HALL.

6. ANN FISH, born 1740, died ————. Married, 1765, ROBERT FREE-
   BORN.

7. RUTH FISH, born 1742, died 1818. Married, 1761, SAMPSON SHERMAN.

8. ROBERT FISH, born 1743, died ————. Married 1763, BATHSHEBA
   BARKER.

9. ISAAC FISH, born 1744, died 1779. Married, 1764, RUTH GRINNELL.

10. STEPHEN FISH, born 1746, died ————. Married 1771, JOANNA
    PADDOCK.

11. JOSEPH FISH, born 1747, died 1779. Married ————.

12. PRESERVED FISH, born 1748, died ————. Married, 1769, SARAH
    LAWTON.

13. SUSAANA FISH, born 1749, died 1820. Married, 1768, STEPHEN
    BROWNELL.

14. ELIZABETH FISH, born 1751, died ————. Married, 1769, NATHAN
    BROWNELL.

15. ————, a son, born 1751, twin of ELIZABETH, died in infancy.

16. PATIENCE FISH, born 1753, died 1831. Married, 1783, JEREMIAH
    AUSTIN.

VIII. ELIZABETH, No. 14 above, married NATHAN BROWN-
ELL. For the continuation of this record see the Brownell
Family.

HALL

I. WILLIAM HALL, of Newport and Portsmouth, R. I., on the 8th day of the 8th month in 1638 was one of fifty-nine persons admitted inhabitants of an island, just off the coast of Rhode Island, now called, "Aquedunk." In 1639 he was an inhabtant of Newport, R. I. On the 27th day of the 5th month in 1644 a piece of land in Portsmouth, R. I., was granted to him and his name appears on the list of freemen there in 1655. He sold land in Portsmouth to Richard Sisson in 1654. He was Commissioner to the General Court from Portsmouth in years 1654 to 1663. He was Deputy to the General Court 1665 to 1673. In 1673 he was appointed Commissioner to treat with the Indians about drunkenness and to seriously counsel with them and if possible find some way to prevent excessive use of intoxicating liquors among them. Five Chiefs are named among which is found the name of "Philip of Mt. Hope" (King Philip of "King Philip's War" fame). We have a trans-atlantic trace of William Hall's ancestry in one, William Hall, a clergyman of London. He was an author and writer who continued the "Fabyon Chronicle," begun by Sir Thomas More. There is reason to believe a connection existed between him and the family of the Lord Chancellor's. This Clement, a near relative of the Mores, was an original founder of Portsmouth, R. I., and was a neighbor of William Hall's. From his will, made in 1673 (Nov. 20), we gather the following record of his family. His wife's name was Mary. Their children were:

1. ZURIEL HALL, born ————, died 1691. Married ELIZABETH TRIPP.

2. BENJAMIN HALL, born ————, died ————. Married FRANCES PARKER.

3. WILLIAM HALL, born ————, died ————. Married ALICE TRIPP.

4. ELIZABETH HALL, born ———, died ———. Married ———.

5. REBECCA HALL, born ———, died ———. Married ———.

6. DELIVERANCE HALL, born ———, died ———. Married ABIEL TRIPP.

II. ZURIEL HALL, No. 1 above, born ———; died 1691. Married Elizabeth Tripp, daughter of John and Mary (Paine) Tripp and sister of Abiel, who married Deliverance, No. 6 above. Zuriel and Elizabeth had the following children:

1. MARY HALL, born ———, died ———. Married ROBERT FISH.

2. ZURIEL HALL, born ———, died ———. Married HANNAH SHEFFIELD.

II. DELIVERANCE HALL, No. 6 above, born ———; died ———. Married ABIEL TRIPP. For the continuation of this record see Fish Family and Tripp Family of this book.

HAZARD

I. THOMAS HAZARD, the progenitor of the Hazard family in America, was born in 1610 and died in 1680. His name is first found in Boston, Mass., in 1635. He was admitted freeman there in 1638. Two years later he was admitted freeman in Portsmouth, Rhode Island. In 1639, April 28, with ten others, he signed a contract preparatory to the settlement of Newport, R. I. The first officers of the town were: Nicholas Eaton, Judge; John Coggeshall, William Brenton, John Clark, Jeremy Clark, THOMAS HAZARD and Henry Bull, elders; Wiliam Dyer, Clerk. In 1639 he was named one of the four proportioners of land in Newport. In 1640 he was a member of the General Court of Elections. In 1665 he was for a short time in Newtown, Long Island. His will was proved in 1680. In it he names his wife, Martha, whom he calls his "Yoke fellow," his sole executrix, and gives her his whole estate. He was married twice, both wives bearing the same name, Martha. His children were:

1. ROBERT HAZARD, born in England, 1635; died 1710. Married MARY BROWNELL.

2. ELIZABETH HAZARD, born ————, died ————. Married GEORGE LAWTON.

3. HANNAH HAZARD, born ————, died ————. Married STEPHEN WILCOX.

4. MARTHA HAZARD, born ————, died ————. Married, first, ICHABOD POTTER; second, BENJAMIN MOURY.

II. ELIZABETH HAZARD, No. 2 above. Married GEORGE LAWTON. For the continuation of this record see "Lawton."

HAZEN

The following record is taken from "The Hazen Family," Four American Generations, by Henry Allen Hazen, of New Haven, Conn.

I. EDWARD HAZEN was the Immigrant Ancestor. The first mention of the name found to date occurs in the records of Rowley, Conn., and is as follows: "Elizabeth, the wife of Edward Hasson, was Buryed Sept. 18, 1699. He was a man of substance and influence in the town, being overseer, selectman, and judge from 1650 to 1666. His estate inventoried at 404 pounds."

Of his first wife, Elizabeth, nothing is known. He married for a second wife, HANNAH, daughter of THOMAS and HANNAH (——————) GRANT. He died in Rowley, Conn., July 22, 1683. His widow married again, March 2, 1684, George Bourne, of Haverhill, who adopted her youngest son, Richard, as his sole heir to a very large estate. The children of Edward Hazen and Hannah Grant were:

1. ELIZABETH HAZEN, born March 8, 1651. Married April 1, 1670, NATHANIEL HARRIS.

2. HANNAH HAZEN, born September, 1653. Married WILLIAM GIBSON.

3. JOHN HAZEN, born September, 1655. Unmarried.

4. THOMAS HAZEN, born February, 1657. Married MARY HOWLETT. She died 1735.

5. EDWARD HAZEN, born September, 1660; died 1748.

6. ISABEL HAZEN, born July, 1662. Married JOHN WOOD.

7. PRISCILLA HAZEN, born November, 1664. Married JEREMIAH PEARSON.

8. EDNY HAZEN, born June, 1667. Married TIMOTHY PERKINS.

9. RICHARD HAZEN, born August, 1669; died 1733.

10. HIPHGEBATH HAZEN, born December, 1671. Married and died, 1689.

11. SARAH HAZEN, born 1673. Married DANIEL WICOM.

II. THOMAS HAZEN, No. 4 above. He owned a farm at Rowley at the time of his father's death. He removed to Boxford in 1689, where he was made a freeman. He joined the Church in Boxford by letter from Rowley. In 1711 he removed to Norwich, Conn., where he died April 12, 1735. He married, June 1, 1683, Mary, daughter of Thomas Howlett and granddaughter of Sergeant Thomas Howlett, one of the original settlers of Agawenn, now Ipswich, in 1623. A man of importance in Ipswich. Their children were:

1. JOHN HAZEN, born 1683. Married MARY BRADSTREET.

2. HANNAH HAZEN, born 1684. Married JOSHUA MORSE.

3. ALICE HAZEN, born 1686 .

4. EDNAH HAZEN, born 1688. Married, 1724, JOSHUA SMITH.

5. THOMAS HAZEN, born 1690; died 1776.

6. JACOB HAZEN, born 1692; died 1755.

7. MARY HAZEN, twin, born 1694.

8. LYDIA HAZEN, twin, born 1694.

9. HEPSIBAH HAZEN, born 1697. Married, 1716, DAVID LADD of Norwich.

10. RUTH HAZEN.

11. JEREMIAH HAZEN.

For the continuation of this record, see "LADD" Family.

HOWLETT

0⹀⹀⹀⹀0

I. THOMAS HOWLETT lived in Ipswich, Mass., in 1635. His lot, granted by the Court, was next to Thomas Hardy's in the crossway leading to the Mill. In 1637 he purchased of John Perkins 40 acres of land for 7 pounds, 10 shillings. His name, bearing the title "Ensign," is in the list of those who promise to donate one day's work toward a public bridge. In 1643 Sergeant Howlett and ten soldiers are in service against the Indians. The soldiers received 12 pence per day and the officers double. He was a commoner in 1641. He owned a share and a half in Plum Island in 1668. He was Deputy to the General Court in 1635. He died in 1678, age 79 years. His first wife was ALICE FRENCH. In his will he mentions wife, Rebecca Cummings. His children were:

1. THOMAS HOWLETT, born ————; died 1667. He married MARY PEABODY.

2. SAMUEL HOWLETT, Born ————; died ————.

3. SARAH HOWLETT, born ————; died ————. Married JOHN CUMMINGS.

4. MARY HOWLETT, born ————; died ————. Married ———— PERLEY.

5. NATHANIEL HOWLETT, born ————; died 1658.

6. WILLIAM HOWLETT, born 1650; died ————.

7. JOHN HOWLETT, born ————; died ————.

II. THOMAS HOWLETT, No. 1 above. Married MARY PEABODY. Their children were:

1. MARY HOWLETT, born ————; died ————. Married THOMAS HAZEN.

JENCKS

I. REGINALD JENCKS, or Jenkins, as the name is sometimes
spelled, is found in Dorchester, Mass., in 1630. Two years
later he removed to Cape Porpus and there was killed by the
Indians. He had at least one son, but we have not found any
record of his wife or other children. Perhaps they never came
to this country. His son was:

II. REGINALD JENCKS (in some places it is spelled Reynold
Jenkins). According to his own depositions, he was born in
1608 in England. He was in the service of one, John Winters
of Richmond's Island, during the years 1634 to 1639. From
1647 to 1683 he was living in what is now "Eliot." His wife's
given name was ANN. Their children were:

1. PHILADELPHIA JENCKS, born 1645; died 1721. Married, first, EDWARD
HAYES; second, MATTHEW ESTES.

2. STEPHEN JENCKS, born 1653; died ———. Married, first, ELIZ-
ABETH PITMAN; second, ANN ———.

3. JABEZ JENCKS, born 1655; died ———. Married HANNAH CURTIS.

4. MARY JENCKS, born ———; died ———. Married, 1666, JOHN
GREEN.

5. SARAH JENCKS, born ———; died ———. Married JONATHAN
MASON.

6. JOSEPH JENCKS, born ———; died ———. Married ———.
Lived in Dover, Me.

III. PHILADELPHIA JENCKS, No. 1 above, born 1645; died
1721. Married twice, first, Edward Hayes and, second, MAT-
THEW ESTES, born in Dover, England, in 1645. For a list
of their children and the pedigree of Matthew see "Estes"
Family.

JENKINS

1. RICHARD LEWIS JENKINS was born in Yorkshire, England, October 16, 1791, and died somewhere in, or near, California, July 8, 1853. He had gone out there in 1849 in the "rush for gold" and it has always been believed by his descendants that he met with "foul play," as it is known that he started for home having been quite successful in his prospecting. We do not know just when he came to this country, but it must have been in his youth, for he married here March 30, 1816, ANN MARIA LEAKE. She was born in this country and the family tradition is that she came from Pennsylvania to New York State. They must have lived in Waterloo, N. Y., for their first child, Margaret Lewis Jenkins, was born there. In the old Bible now in possession of the family in Burr Oak, Mich., which belonged to Richard, the following verse is written in his own handwriting:

> "Richard Jenkins is my name,
> England is my nation,
> Jiniva is my dwelling place,
> Christ is my salvation."

"Jiniva" is the way he spelled "Geneva." After thirteen or fourteen years the family migrated to St. Joseph's Co., Mich. The name of the village near which they located is Burr Oak. The children of Richard and Ann Maria were:

1. MARGARET LEWIS JENKINS, born March 18, 1818; died December 15, 1852. Married, November 19, 1833, VERANUS BROWNELL.

2. JOHN THOMAS JENKINS born 1820; died ———. Married, first, 1843, ELIZA KOM; second, HARRIET FELLOWS. Children, by first wife, RICHARD, JOHN, MARGARET, ADALINE and ELLEN JENKINS; by second wife, DELL, SARAH, FREY and GUY JENKINS.

3. JAMES EVAN JENKINS born 1822; died ———. Married, first ———; second, ——— BASSETT. Children, by first wife, GEORGE and MARTHA JENKINS; by second wife, BEATRICE, LEWIS, ALBERT and ROY JENKINS.

4. ELIZABETH BURNETT JENKINS, born 1823; died ————. Married, 1845, ALONZO CROSS. Children:

   a. ELLEN CROSS. Married THANE BLANCHARD.

   b. MARTHA CROSS. Married PHILIP GOODRICH. Moved to Arizona.

   c. WILL CROSS.

5. MARTHA DAVIE JENKINS, born 1825; died ————. Married, 1840, GEORGE MEABON. Children:

   a. MARGARET MEABON; died in infancy.

   b. WILLIAM MEABON; died in infancy.

6. ISAAC NEWTON JENKINS, born 1828; died 1925. Married ELIZA BASSETT, widow. He had no children of his own. She had three children by her first husband. They took good care of him in his old age. He was bed-ridden many years, having had his hip and leg broken by the explosion of a thrashing engine, which killed also his nephew, NELSON JENKINS, son of JOSEPH JENKINS, No. 8 below.

7. LUCENA JENKINS, born 1831; died 1909. Married, 1850, JAMES TOWER. Children: ISAAC, KARL, VIOLA and JOY TOWER. (They live in Roscommon Co., Mich.)

8. JOSEPH JEKINS, born 1833; died 1925. Married, 1856, MARY JANE FELLOWS Children:

   a. NELSON JENKINS.

   b. BURTON JENKINS. He married NETTIE CLAYFORD. (One daughter, CLARISSA JENKINS.

   c. JANE JENKINS. Married HERMAN ZANISTER.

   d. EDITH JENKINS. Married JUDSON CLAYPOOL.

   e. ROY JENKINS. Married MARY TEAL.

   f. IDA MAY JENKINS. Married EDWARD COWLES.

9. DANIEL JENKINS, born 1835; died 1899. Married, 1855, ESTHER ANN COWLES. Children:

   a. PRISCELLA JENKINS. Married, first, WILLIAM BISHOP; second, GENE VAN WORMER, and, third, HOWARD JENKINS. She is now (1926) a widow.

b. CLARA JENKINS. Married CHARL HAGADORN.

c. LUELLA JENKINS. Married HARLOW BOWDITCH.

d. FRANK JENKINS. Married MAGGIE JOHNSON. Two daughters:

  1. *Laverne Jenkins,* married *Verne Shane.*
  2. *Fern Valentine Jenkins,* married *Tray Graydon Thurston.*

10. WILLIAM COLE JENKINS, born 186—, died 1901. Married LUCIA STERNBERG. They had six children and five of them died at one time with scarlet fever and diphtheria. They have one boy left, LEE JENKINS, who lives with his mother in Gratiot Co., Mich. He is married and has four children, all living.

II. MARGARET LEWIS JENKINS, No. 1 above, born March 18, 1818, and died December 15, 1852. She married VERANUS BROWNELL. For a record of their children and his pedigree see "Brownell" Family.

LADD

o=======●

I. DANIEL LADD took the oath of Supremacy and Allegiance to pass to New England in the "Mary and John" of London. Robert Sawyer, Master, the 24th of March, 1634. The first record made of him at his arrival in Ipswich is on February 15, 1637. He was given six acres of land, on which he built a dwelling house. Six years later he sold the property to Henry Kingsbury. He is next found in Salisbury and after a few years he removed to Haverhill, Mass. He married Ann ————, probably about 1639 or '40. But we know nothing further about her. She died February 9, 1694. In Vol. II of the New Hampshire Genealogy, page 867, the statement is made that the name "Ladd," is of French origin, and that Daniel Ladd came from Wiltshire, Eng. He was a Selectman in Haverhill in 1668. (The village of Haverhill is one-half in Massachusetts and the other half in New Hampshire. This explains why it is written either way, i.e. in N. H. or in Mass.) At the outbreak of the King Philip's War, he with two others, was appointed to designate which houses should be garrisoned. His will was dated in 1692 and he died July 27, 1693. The children were:

1. ELIZABETH LADD, born 1640; died ————. Married, 1663, NATHANIEL SMITH.

2. DANIEL LADD, born 1642; died ————. Married LYDIA SINGLETREE.

3. LYDIA LADD, born 1645; died ————. Married JOSIAH GAGE.

4. MARY LADD, born 1646; died ————. Married. 1682, CALEB RICHARDSON.

5. SAMUEL LADD, born 1649; died 1697. Married MARY CORLISS.

6. NATHANIEL LADD, born 1651; died ————. Married ELIZABETH GILMAN.

7. EZEKIEL LADD, born 1654; died ————. Married MARY FOLSOM.

8. SARAH LADD, born 1657; died ————. Married, 1685, ONESIPHORUS MARSH.

II. SAMUEL LADD, No. 5 above, born in Haverhill, November 1, 1649, and died in 1697. These records and the record of his marriage (Dec. 1, 1674, to MARY CORLISS) may be seen in the Haverhill records. Their children were:

1. DANIEL LADD, born 1675; died 1675.

2. DANIEL LADD, born 1676; died 1751. Married SUSANNA HARTSHORN.

3. LYDIA LADD, born 1679; died 1684.

4. SAMUEL LADD, born 1682; died ————. Married HANNAH HARTSHORN.

5. NATHANIEL LADD, born 1684; died ————. Married ————.

6. EZEKIEL LADD, born 1685; died ————. Married ————.

7. DAVID LADD, born 1689; died 1728. Married HEPZIBAH HAZEN.

8. JONATHAN LADD, twin of DAVID LADD; died ————. Married ————.

9. ABIGAIL LADD, born 1691; died ————. Married SAMUEL ROBERDS.

10. JOHN LADD, born 1694; died ————. Married MARY MORILL.

11. JOSEPH LADD, born 1697; died 1697.

III. DAVID LADD, No. 7 above. Married in Norwich, Conn., to Hepzibah Hazen. Had following issue:

1. AZUBAH LADD, born 1717; died ————. Married DANIEL ALLEN.

2. HEPZIBAH LADD, born 1719; died ————. Married ELIAKIM PERRY.

3. BATHSHEBA LADD, born 1721; died ————. Married ABIJAH SMITH.

4. JEREMIAH LADD, born 1723; died ————. Married JERUSHA SABIN.

5. HANNAH LADD, born 1725; died ————. Married ————.

6. DAVID LADD, born 1727; died ————. Married MARY WALBRIDGE.

IV. AZUBAH LADD, No. 1 above, born 1717, November 3. Married, October 3, 1741, to DANIEL ALLEN, son of TIMOTHY ALLEN and RACHEL BUSHNELL. The Allens lived in Bridgewater, Mass., for several generations. Azubah and Daniel lived in Norwich and Ashford, Conn. For a continuation of this record, giving their children and his pedigree, see "Allen" Family.

LAWTON

The Lawton provides a lineage of historic Cheshire, England. It was founded in the time of the "Conqueror," when the Norman progenitor of the family acquired large landed estates, and bestowed his name on the territory. A long and ancient pedigree of the family exists since the reign of Henry VI (1165-1197) when Hugh de Lawton of Cheshire is found in possession of the Manor of Lawton in that country, his inheritance from his early ancestors.

I. HUGH de LAWTON, Cheshire, England, living in the latter part of the 12th Century, married ISABELLA KERNYS, daughter of John Modoe and the widow of Bekyn Kernys, the heiress of Modoe.

II. JOHN de LAWTON, surviving son of Hugh and Isabella (Modoe-Kernys) de Lawton, died before his father, having been married and left one son only, viz:

III. RICHARD LAWTON, Esq., Cheshire, heir of the Manor of Lawton. Left a son,

IV. JAMES LAWTON, Esq., Cheshire, married ELEANOR MOORE, daughter of Matthew Moore of "Hall o' the Heath," or "Halloheath." Left a son,

V. WILLIAM LAWTON, Esq., Cheshire, married KATHERINE BELLOT, daughter of Thomas Bellot, Esq., of Moreton Co., Chester. He died in the 5th year of the reign of Edward VI, viz, 1542. He left, among other children,

VI. JOHN LAWTON, of Lawton, Cheshire, England. He was living in the manor in 1580. He married, first, Anne Corbet, widow of Robert Corbet; no issue. He married, second, Margaret Dutton, daughter of Fulke Dutton, Esq. Left a son,

VII. JOHN LAWTON, of Lawton, Cheshire, England. Youngest child and fourth son, born 1582. Married ————. They had three sons, all of whom came to America—viz: John Lawton, George Lawton and THOMAS LAWTON. They settled in Portsmouth, R. I.

VIII. THOMAS LAWTON married Grace Bailey, daughter of Hugh and Elizabeth (————) Bailey. He was one of the signers of the "Portsmouth Compact." They had the following children, all born in Portsmouth, R. I.:

1. ELIZABETH LAWTON, born ————; died 1711. Married PELEG SHERMAN (1638-1719).

2. DANIEL LAWTON, born ————; died 1719. Married REBECCA ————.

3. ANN LAWTON, born ————; died ————. Married GILES SLOCUM.

4. SARAH LAWTON, born ————; died 1718. Married GEORGE SISSON.

5. ISAAC LAWTON, born 1650; died 1732. Married, first MARY SISSON; second, ELIZABETH TALLMAN.

6. NAOMI LAWTON, born ————; died ————. Married ————.

IX. ISAAC LAWTON, No. 5 above. No children by first wife. Had following by second wife:

1. ELIZABETH LAWTON, born 1675; died ————. Married ————.

2. SARAH LAWTON, born 1676; died ————. Married ————.

3. ANN LAWTON, born 1678; died ————. Married ————.

4. ISAAC LAWTON, born 1681; died ————. Married ————.

5. MARY LAWTON, born 1683; died ————. Married ————.

6. ISABEL LAWTON, born 1685; died ————. Married ————.

7. THOMAS LAWTON, born 1687; died ————. Married ————.

8. Susanna Lawton, born 1689; died ————. Married Thomas Cornell.

9. Job Lawton, born 1691; died ————. Married ————.

10. Ruth Lawton, born 1694; died ————. Married ————.

11. John Lawton, born 1696; died ————. Married ————.

For continuation of this record, see "Cornell" Family.

LEFFINGWELL

I. THOMAS LEFFINGWELL was born in England in 1620 and
died in 1712, being 92 years of age. The earliest record of him
in this country is found in Saybrook, Conn., in 1637. He was
a freeman of that place and in very important matters of general interest was intimately associated with Matthew Griswold.
He also was a people's Advocate and Defender. He stood for
the rights of the Indians (Mohegans). For this reason he and
his people were saved from hostile attacks. This tribe gave
him a deed to the whole of Norwich, Conn., a township nine
miles square. He removed from Saybrook to Norwich in 1659.
He held the offices of Sargent, Lieutenant and Ensign. He was
Representative to the State General Court, and was in actual at-
tendance at Hartford during fifty-six sessions prior to and including 1700. In 1704 he was appointed Captain of Queen
Ann's Royal Commissioners, being associated with Governor
Dudley of Massachusetts, Thomas Hooker of Hartford, James
Avery and John Morgan of New London. He was a member
of the First Church during the pastorate of Rev. Mr. Fitch,
taking a prominent part in the work thereof. He ranked high
among the real estate owners of the day, holding extensive
tracts of land. He divided his property among his heirs prior
to his death. He married in England MARY WHITE. She
died in Norwich, Conn., February 6, 1711. Their children were:

1. RACHEL LEFFINGWELL, born 1648; died ————. Married, 1681, ROB-
ERT PARKE.

2. THOMAS LEFFINGWELL, born 1649; died 1724. Married MARY BUSH-
NELL.

3. JONATHAN LEFFINGWELL, born 1650; died ————. Married ————.

4. JOSEPH LEFFINGWELL, born 1652; died ————. Married ————.

5. MARY LEFFINGWELL, born 1654; died 1745. Married JOSEPH BUSH-NELL.

6. NATHANIEL LEFFINGWELL, born 1656; died ————. Married MARY SMITH.

7. SAMUEL LEFFINGWELL, born 1661; died ————. Married ANNA DICKENSON.

For the continuation of this record and the BUSHNELL pedigree, see "BUSHNELL Family."

MARVIN

0━━━━━0

The English home of the Marvin Family more than a century and a half before the emigration of Reinold and Matthew Marvin to this country was in the Northeastern part of the County of Essex. A century before that we find several Marvin families living only about ten miles north of the home of the Grandfather of the emigrant brothers.

In the Church of St. Michael the Archangel, built in the days of the Normans (about 1100 A. D.), with its massive square tower of Purbeck Stone, green the year around with never fading ivy, Rynalde Marvin, the above name Grandfather, in his will dated December 22, 1554, bequeaths his "Soule to Almyhte God, My Maker." Directs that his body be "buryed" in the Aisle North of the Chancel. His signature to this will, which is preserved in Somerset House, London, is given in facsimile here.

A little more than two miles west of Ramsey Bridge stands the house which for several centuries has been known as the "Mravin Home." Here

1. RYNALDE MARVIN lived and died, leaving the Ancestral Home to his son,

   1. EDWARD MARVIN, born 1550, eldest son.

   2. RICHARD MARVIN, born 1552. Inherited the property known as Bennetts.

   3. JOHN MARVIN, born ————. Inherited the property known as Gannets.

   4. AUDRE MARVIN.

5. MARGARET MARVIN.

6. BARBARA MARVIN.

The three girls inherited 10 pounds each.

II. EDWARD MARVIN, No. 1 above, born 1550, died November 14, 1615. His wife's given name was Margaret. She died May 28, 1633. He must have moved from Ramsey to Great Bentley as his older children were born at the former place and the two youngest were born at Great Bentley. The children were:

1. EDWARD MARVIN, born 1581. See below.

2. THOMAS MARVIN, born 1583; died 1651.

2. RICHARD MARVIN, born 1585; died ————.

4. ROBERT MARVIN, born 1587; died ————.

5. MARGARET MARVIN, born 1589; at Great Bentley "Jan'y, ye 28th day, 1596."

6. MARIE MARVIN, born 1591. Married, first, JOHN HAYS; second, RICHARD WOOD.

7. JOHN MARVIN, twin, born June 7, 1593; died the same day.

8. REINOLD MARVIN, twin, born June 7, 1593; died the same day.

9. RENOLD MARVIN, born 1594. The ancestor of REINOLD Line in America.

10. ELIZABETH MARVIN, born 1597. Married ROBERT EDWARDS.

11. MATTHEW MARVIN, born 1600, March 26. He was the ancestor of the MATTHEW Line in America.

III. MATTHEW MARVIN, No. 11 above. His father's will gave him "The Mentchon (Mansion) House," called "Edon's," or "Dreybrockes." Also lands and other property. He was 15 years old when his father died. He continued to live in this old home until his mother's death in 1633. The house, or Mansion, is still standing. Matthew married, in 1622, Elizabeth, born 1604 and died in Hartford, Conn., 1640. He married, second, Alice, widow of John Bouton. Matthew, with wife Elizabeth and four children came to America in Ship "Increase," in the year 1635. Robert Lee Master. He made affidavit at that time that he was 35 years of age, and that wife Elizabeth was 31. Their children were:

1. ELIZABETH MARVIN, born 1624. Came in New England with her father in 1635. She married DR. JOHN OLMSTED and lived in Norwich.

2. MATTHEW MARVIN, born 1627. Came to this country with his parents. His wife's name was MARY.

3. MARY MARVIN, born 1629. Came to this country with her parents. She died in Norwich, March 29, 1713. Age 84. See below.

4. SARAH MARVIN, born 1632. Married WILLIAM GOODRICH.

5. HANNAH MARVIN, born 1634. Married THOMAS SEYMOUR.

6. ABIGAIL MARVIN, born ————. Married JOHN BOUTON.

7. RACHEL MARVIN, born 1649. Married SAMUEL SMITH.

IV. MARY MARVIN, No. 3 above. Married in 1648, Richard Bushnell. For the continuation of this record see "Bushnell" Family.

PARTRIDGE

0━━━━━0

The name has been variously spelled: "Partrich," "Partick," or even "Patrick" are some of queerest forms.

I. GEORGE PARTRIDGE was a "Yeoman" and one of the most respectable in the colony. He came from the county of Kent, England, in 1636. He owned an estate in Kent which he mentions in his will. He received a grant of land at Powder Point the year of his arrival in this country, with permission to build a house there. The next year he was allowed 20 acres at Green Harbor Path and the following year 30 acres more at Island Creek and at the same place in 1666 he received 40 acres additional. Also in 1668, 50 acres more at Mill Brook. This parcel of land he sold to Thomas King, Jr., of Scituate, two years later. He was admitted a Freeman in 1646. His will, dated June 26, 1682, was witnessed by Alexander and Josiah Standish. He died soon thereafter. He married in November, 1638, SARAH TRACY, daughter of Stephen Tracy, of Plymouth. See "Tracy" Family. Their children were:

1. SARAH PARTRIDGE, born 1639; died ————. Married DEACON SAMUEL ALLEN, Bridgewater.

2. JOHN PARTRIDGE, born ————; died ————. Married, first, 1684, HANNAH SEABURY; second, MARY BREWSTER.

3. LYDIA PARTRIDGE, born ————; died 1743. Married DEACON WILLIAM BREWSTER.

4. RUTH PARTRIDGE, born ————; died ————. Married, 1670, RUDOLPHUS THATCHER.

5. TRYPHOSA PARTRIDGE, born ————; died ————. Married, 1668, SAMUEL WEST.

6. MERCY PARTRIDGE, born ————; died ————. Married ————.

7. James Partridge, born ———; died 1745. Married ———.

Note: George Partridge was a brother of the Rev. Ralph Partridge, the first minister of Duxbury, first arrived in Boston, 1636. He came from Kent, England, where he was many years a minister at Sutton, near Dover.

For the continuation of this record and the pedigree of Deacon Samuel Allen, see "Allen" Family.

SWAIN

I. RICHARD SWAIN came to America in the "Truelove" in 1635, being at that time 34 years old. He settled first in Hampton, N. H. His wife, Elizabeth, came over a little later in the "Planter," and his sons, William and Francis, in the "Rebecca," and his daughters, Elizabeth, Susan and Ellen, under the care of various friends. His house lot in Rowley, whither he moved after a few years, was on both sides of the cove formed by the Northwest extension of the Hammock Pond. He performed official duties for the town in regard to sheep and cattle. After his first wife's death he married, June, widow of George Bunker, in 1658.

II. JOHN SWAIN, son of Richard by his first wife, Elizabeth, was one of the original proprietors of Nantucket. He lived in Polpis, on the island. His house was standing until 1902, where it was struck by lightning and destroyed. He married MARY WYER, daughter of Nathaniel Wyer and Sarah ———, his wife. He died in 1717. His children were:

1. MARY SWAIN, born ———; died ———. Married JOSEPH NASON.

2. JOHN SWAIN, born 1664; died ———. Married EXPERIENCE FOLGER (PETER).

3. STEPHEN SWAIN, born 1666; died ———.

4. SARAH SWAIN, born 1670; died ———. Married JOSEPH NORTON.

5. JOSEPH SWAIN, born 1673; died ———. Married MARAH SIBLEY.

6. ELIZABETH SWAIN, born 1676; died ———. Married JOSHUA SEVOLLE.

7. BENJAMIN SWAIN, born 1679; died ——— Married MARY TAYLOR.

8. HANNAH SWAIN, born ———; died ———. Married JOSEPH TALLMAN.

9. PATIENCE SWAIN, born ———; died ———. Married SAMUEL GARDNER.

For the continuation of this line see "TALLMAN" Family.

TALLMAN

1. PETER TALLMAN came to this country from England and settled in Newport and Portsmouth, R. I. He was made a Freeman in 1655. In 1658 he bought 9 acres of land for 35 shillings an acre. In 1661 he was General Solicitor for R. I. and Commissioner in 1662. He was Deputy Governor 1662 to 1665. In 1655 he was granted a divorce from his wife, Ann. He was married three times, as follows; first, Ann; second, JOAN BRIGGS, born ————, died 1685; third, Esther, born ————, died 1708. He made a pre-nuptial agreement with Joan Briggs in which he agreed to give her a house and lot to be hers and her heirs, born to this union, forever. Also to give her a bed and one-half the household furniture. But if she should die without issue, then all these things should revert to Peter's oldest daughter by his first wife, Ann, viz, Mary, and her heirs. He gave Joan also, as a free gift, three good cows and a good breeding mare. His children were:

1. MARY TALLMAN, born ————; died 1720. Married JOHN PEARCE, born 1647; died 1707, son of RICHARD and SUSANNA PEARCE.

2. ELIZABETH TALLMAN, born ————; died 1701. Married, 1674, ISAAC LAWTON.

3. PETER TALLMAN, born 1658; died 1726. Married, 1683, ANN WALSTONE.

4. ANN TALLMAN, born ————; died ————. Married, 1679, STEPHEN BRAYTON.

5. JOSEPH TALLMAN, no record.

6. SUSANNA TALLMAN. Married ———— BECKETT.

7. A daughter. Married WILLIAM WILBER.

8. JONATHAN TALLMAN, born ————; died 1762. Married SARAH ————.

9. JAMES TALLMAN, born ————; died 1724. Married, first, MARY DEVOL; second, HANNAH SWAIN. See below.

10. A daughter. Married WILLIAM POTTER.

11. JOHN TALLMAN, born ————; died 1709. Married MARY ————.

12. A daughter. Married ISRAEL SHAW.

13. BENJAMIN TALLMAN, born 1684; died 1759. Married, first, PATIENCE DURFEE and, second, DEBORAH COOK.

14. SAMUEL TALLMAN, born 1688; died ————.

II. JAMES TALLMAN, No. 9 above. He was a physician. He deeded to Mary Timberlake some land for kindnesses to him shown. He deeded to brother, Benjamin, Samuel and Joseph, for love, etc., 12 acres each. The will of one, Thomas Barnes, ordered his debts paid, "especially to my careful and kind Doctor, James Tallman," etc.

His will was proved in February, 1724, wife, Hannah, Executrix. Estate inventoried at 1373 pounds. A very large estate.

His widow was also a practicing physician and continued her profession until her death in September, 1765. Beside other bequests she left 600 pounds to her daughter, Jemina Fish. Children by first wife:

1. JOHN TALLMAN, born 1692.

2. JOSEPH TALLMAN, born 1694.

3. ELIZABETH TALLMAN, born 1699.
    First wife died. Children by second wife:

4. STEPHEN TALLMAN, born 1702.

5. MARY TALLMAN, born 1704.

6. PETER TALLMAN, born 1706.

7. JEMIMA TALLMAN, born September 11, 1708. Married, 1730, DAVID FISH.

8. JAMES TALLMAN, born 1710.

9. JEREMIAH TALLMAN, born 1712.

10. SILAS TALLMAN, born 1717.

11. JOSEPH TALLMAN, born 1720.

12. HANNAH TALLMAN, born 1723.

For continuation of this record see "FISH" Family.

TRACY

I. STEPHEN TRACY was in Plymouth in 1623 and in Duxbury in 1639. He returned to England before 1654, for in the Colonial records we find a disposition of his property in New England, dated London, March 20, 1654. Empowering John Winslow to make the transactions. He calls himself of St. Yarmouth, England, and says he had five children living in New England. His wife's name was Tryphosa ————. They were married in Leyden, January 2, 1621, where the Dutch record has her name spelled Tryfosa, and the surname is illegible. Their children were:

1. JOHN (Ensign) TRACY of Duxbury, born ————; died 1701. Married, first, MARY PRENCE and, second, DEBORAH ————.

2. THOMAS (Lieut.) TRACY, born ————; died ————. Married ————.

3. RUTH TRACY, born ————; died ————. Married ————.

4. MARY TRACY, born ————; died ————. Married CULLIFER ————.

5. SARAH TRACY, born in England, probably the eldest child. Married GEORGE PARTRIDGE.

II. SARAH TRACY, No. 5 above. Married in November, 1638, GEORGE PARTRIDGE, probably a brother of Rev. Ralph Partridge, the first minister of Duxbury. For a continuation of this record see "Partridge" Family.

TRIPP

I. JOHN TRIPP, SR., born in England in 1610 and died in Portsmouth, R. I., in 1678. He was Deputy Governor from 1648 to 1669, inclusive. He went to Rhode Island with Roger Williams for conscience sake. His wife was MARY PAINE, daughter of ANTHONY and ROSE GRINNELL PAINE. (She was a widow.) Mary Paine was born ————, and died 1687. Their children were:

1. JOHN TRIPP, born 1640; died 1719. Married SUSANNA ANTHONY.

2. PELEG TRIPP, born 1641; died 1713. Married ANNA SISSON.

3. JOSEPH TRIPP, born 1644; died ————. Married MEHITABLE FISH.

4. MARY TRIPP, born 1646; died 1716. Married, first GERSHORN WODELL; second, JONATHAN GETCHEL.

5. ELIZABETH TRIPP, born 1648; died 1670. Married ZURIEL HALL.

6. ALICE TRIPP, born 1650; died ————. Married WILLIAM HALL.

7. ISABEL TRIPP, born 1651; died 1716. Married SAMPSON SHERMAN.

8. ABIEL TRIPP, born 1653; died 1684. Married DELIVERANCE HALL.

9. JAMES TRIPP, born 1656; died 1730. Married, first, MERCY LAWTON; second, ELIZABETH CUDWORTH.

10. MARTHA TRIPP, born 1658; died 1717. Married SAMUEL SHERMAN.

II. ELIZABETH TRIPP, No. 5 above, born 1648, died 1670. Married Zuriel Hall. For the record of their children and his pedigree see "Hall" Family.

II. ABIEL TRIPP, No. 8 above, born 1653, died 1684. Married

Deliverance Hall, sister of above Zuriel. They were married in 1679 and their only child that lived was

1. ABIEL TRIPP, born 1684, the year of the death of the father.

III. ABIEL TRIPP, born 1684, died ————. Married Elinor Wait, daughter of Reuben Wait and Tabitha Lounders. They were married 1703 and had the following eleven children:

1. WAIT TRIPP, born 1705; died ————. Married ————.

2. ABIEL TRIPP, born 1707; died ————. Married ————.

3. MARY TRIPP, born 1710; died ————. Married ————.

4. SARAH TRIPP, born 1712; died ————. Married ————.

5. ELEANOR TRIPP, born 1715; died ————. Married ————.

6. JOSEPH TRIPP, born 1717; died ————. Married ————.

7. REBECCA TRIPP, born 1719; died ————. Married JOSEPH BROWN-ELL.

8. THOMAS TRIPP, born 1721; died ————. Married ————.

9. ELIZABETH TRIPP, born 1724; died ————. Married ————.

10. Infant, born 1726.

11. AMY TRIPP, born 1728; died ————. Married ————.

IV. REBECCA TRIP, No. 7 above, born 1719, died ————. Married JOSEPH BROWNELL. For list of their children and his pedigree see "Brownell" Family.

WAIT

The name was originally spelled Wayghte, and is derived from an old Anglo Saxon word meaning, to watch. The first Waits were found in England at the time of the Norman Conquest. William, the Conqueror, gave the Earldom of Norwich to Ralf de Waiet in 1075 A. D. He was the son of Rolf, who married "Emma," a cousin of the Conqueror. She was named after her great-aunt, Queen Emma, who was the wife of two kings and the mother of two kings. William the Conqueror was the son of Richard, the 4th Duke of Normandy, and grandson of Richard the 3rd Duke of Normandy and great-grandson of William, the 2nd Duke of Normandy, and the 2nd great-grandson of Realf, the 1st Duke of Normandy. The early Waites in England were wandering minstrels. The bugles on their Coat of Arms denote their musical tendencies. They were minstrels and musicians to the King and to his Knights. The earliest settlers in New England by this name were brothers by the name of Richard, born 1596, who was Marshall of Boston, and Gamiel, born 1598 of Boston, and

I. THOMAS WAITE, born 1601, lived in Portsmouth, R. I., and died in 1669. On his arrival in 1639 he applied for land, and at their first meeting thereafter they granted him a house lot. There he lived and the following children were listed as his heirs by the council, he having left no will. (His wife's name was Eleanor.)

1. SAMUEL WAIT.

2. JOSEPH WAIT.

3. JEREMIAH WAIT, born 1648; died 1677. Married MARTHA BROWNELL.

4. GEORGE WAIT.

5. REUBEN WAIT, born ————. Married TABITHA LOUNDERS. (See below.)

6. BENJAMIN WAIT, born 1647, of Hatfield. Married MARTHA. In 1677 she with three children was captured by the Indians. When he recaptured them he found that a daughter had been born. She was named CANADA, as she was born in that country. BENJAMIN WAIT was killed by the Indians, February 29, 1704.

II. REUBEN WAIT, No. 5 above. Married in 1681 TABITHA LOUNDERS, daughter of JOHN LOUNDERS and JANE KIRBY. They both died in the year 1707. Their children were:

1. THOMAS WAIT, born 1683. Married MARY TRIPP.

2. ELEANOR WAIT, born 1688. Married ABIEL TRIPP.

3. BENJAMIN WAIT, born 1690; died unmarried.

4. JOSEPH WAIT, born 1693. Married ELIZ. WOLF.

5. ABIGAIL WAIT, born 1693, twin of JOSEPH; died unmarried.

6. REUBEN WAIT, born 1695. Married ELIZ. HATHAWAY.

7. TABITHA WAIT, born 1695, twin of REUBEN; died unmarried.

8. JEREMIAH WAIT, born 1698; died unmarried.

For the continuation of this record see the "TRIPP" Family.

INDEX

FIGURES REFER TO THE PAGES

om